Life Skills

Speech and Language

Enrichment Activities

English and Spanish Lesson Plans for Children

with Significant Impairments

Volume 2

Animals in Their Homes | City and Country

Seasons and the Sky

Patricia Villarreal, M.S.,CCC-SLP

Bilinguistics, Inc.

Copyright © 2016 Bilinguistics, Inc.

All rights reserved. Printed in the U.S.A.

Published by Bilinguistics, Inc.

1505 Koenig Lane, Austin, TX 78756

For more information, contact Bilinguistics, Inc. or visit us at: www.bilinguistics.com.

Library of Congress Cataloging-in-Publication Data

ISBN-13: 978-0692649039

ISBN-10: 0692649034

ACKNOWLEDGEMENTS

These lesson plans began with an idea that was supported and cultivated by the team of speech-language pathologists at Bilinguistics. Together, we developed materials for each unit based on evidence-based practices and our own clinical expertise. It is our hope that speech-language pathologists, educational professionals, and parents will use these lessons as a means to more closely collaborate to improve the communication skills of students with significant impairments.

We owe a debt of gratitude to the school districts in Central Texas that enabled us to implement the research that became this book. These lesson plans were field-tested with students with a variety of impairments across many academic settings. They have been tweaked and honed to be effective, fun, and efficient. Most importantly, using these lessons in the classrooms allowed us to align each theme with academic curriculum.

Special thanks to Dr. Ellen Kester and Scott Prath for their encouragement and support through the process of developing this book. I also wish to thank Anna Ubels, Kristin Sankovich, Alisa Baron, Emmy Kolanko, Mary Bauman, Jissel Anaya, Farinam Pletka, Hayden Lambert and Maritza Jacobs for their efforts in designing and creating materials. It has truly been a labor of love!

Sincerely,

Patricia Villarreal, M.S., CCC-SLP

FOREWORD

In our work as speech-language pathologists, we have found great challenges in working with the students in life skills classrooms. These classrooms, also referred to as Functional Life Skills, Functional Communication Classes, Structured Learning Centers, and Low-Incidence Classrooms, are generally self-contained classes in which students are separated from the general education population for a portion or all of their day in order to receive the support that they need to be successful in their community.

Students in elementary life skills classrooms are generally between 6 and 12 years of age and they have one or more of the following disabilities:

- ➢ Orthopedic Impairment (OI)

- ➢ Other Health Impairment (OHI)

- ➢ Intellectual Disability (ID)

- ➢ Emotional Disturbance (ED)

- ➢ Learning Disability (LD)

- ➢ Speech Impairment (SI)

- ➢ Autism (AU)

- ➢ Traumatic Brain Injury (TBI)

- ➢ Auditory Impairment (AI)

- ➢ Visual Impairment (VI)

Although these children have a severe level of impairment, it is our responsibility as professionals to expose them to age-appropriate material and content regardless of their level of functioning (ASHA, 2010). The seeming disconnect between the rigor of the academic curriculum and the overall communication levels of these children can be overwhelming. Language skills are the foundation of learning and it is our job to bridge the gap between a student's current language skills and the way academic material is presented so that students are able to learn new concepts and participate to their fullest potential in the academic setting.

The need to bridge the gap between communication skills and academic material for children with profound disabilities drove our goal to create effective intervention units that can address the unique needs of several students in the same session. We needed intervention plans that not only contained content consistent with the school-based curriculum, but that could be easily modified, both physically and linguistically. This was the catapult for the development of our communication units for children with profound disabilities.

We have created this book to share our experiences with you. We constructed and field tested a series of curriculum-based sessions that introduce age-appropriate concepts and modifications for a wide range of disabilities. Our theme-based units make it easy for speech-language pathologists and teachers to incorporate the requirements outlined in the Texas Essential Knowledge and Skills and the Common Core Standards curriculum with appropriate modifications for all students. These units were created, tested, changed, edited, added to and honed by our team of speech-language pathologists. Now, we want to share them with you.

Enjoy and watch your students' communication skills grow!

Best Regards,

The Bilinguistics Team

CONTENTS

FREE YOURSELF FROM THE CHALLENGES OF THE LIFE SKILLS CLASSROOM

For those of us who have had the opportunity to work in a life skills classroom, we know that it can be the most rewarding and most challenging experience. The problem is that this situation is almost always heavily weighted toward the challenging end of the spectrum. But does it have to be?

In a project we began in the elementary schools, we asked ourselves what the most difficult aspects of working in a life skills classroom are. These are not going to be unfamiliar to you.

- Wide range of impairments (cognitive, physical, behavioral, etc.)

- Variety of communication abilities

- Variety of student schedules due to educational needs

- Lack of age-appropriate materials/content to meet student needs

What makes life skills intervention so hard?

It is the fact that we can rarely produce intervention materials that can be used again and again because each activity has to be individually modified for each student. The degree of severity across students differs radically. And what about considering augmentative communication, hearing loss, low vision, and reduced mobility? Therein lies the dilemma.

Can we increase efficiency and effectiveness in life skills intervention?

The answer lies in the lesson planning itself. Materials may not work with all of your students and definitely not with all of the students you will have next year. Generating specific intervention activities is effective in the general education setting but with regards to life skills, we just need to set this idea down. What we can do is 1) create generalized therapy materials around an academic topic and 2) create a spectrum of ways to modify each activity.

What should we focus on?

We are awash in information on goals, curriculum-based intervention, and inclusion. We make powerful materials that we re-employ each year and that only get better as we add to them. It would be a waste of time if we could never use them again. We need to collectively make a pact to retain resources and improve upon our intervention so that our professions can move forward. That is what this book is designed to do.

"An important, but often forgotten element of all lesson plans should be the question, 'Am I excited about this?'"

- Dave Guymon

HOW TO CREATE IMPACTFUL INTERVENTION

How do we make our services and support relevant to students in the school setting? The answer lies in the school curriculum. Research indicates that when teachers and speech-language pathologists collaborate and use classroom content, students make greater gains in their communication skills (Throneburg, Calvert, Sturm, Paramboukas, & Paul, 2000). When we improve students' abilities to communicate their thoughts and ideas on topics that are at the heart of classroom discussions, we are improving their abilities to actively participate in their community.

Collaborate

Large group activities involving the whole class have been shown to be beneficial for students, teachers, and speech-language pathologists (SLPs) (Throneburg et al., 2000). Teachers are able to see examples of how SLPs implement language strategies in a more natural classroom context. SLPs have the opportunity to be a part of the implementation of the academic curriculum. Most importantly, students in collaborative classrooms make progress in communication and academic skills.

Observe

Modifying lesson plans and intervention materials for children with different levels of communication abilities and multiple impairments is a challenging task. When planning for a diverse group of students, it is important to observe students in their classroom setting. Observing will provide insight into the classroom dynamic and the various levels of functioning of the students.

Group Students

Choose which students require individual attention and which students would benefit from being part of a group based on your observations, their speech-language goals, and their communication abilities. Communication abilities can be broken down into:

- Non-verbal

- Non-verbal and intentional with gestures

- Low-verbal (1-2 word utterances)

- Verbal

Design Intervention Session

Intervention can be provided in a variety of formats, including large group (whole class) sessions, small group sessions, and working one-on-one. In our clinical experience, many students benefit from a combination of formats. Breaking up sessions into 15-minute increments is effective because it allows us to target individualized goals and provide opportunities for generalization in groups. For example, a large group "warm-up" routine, in which all the children in the class can participate, can be used to introduce a new concept, theme, or vocabulary. The large group format also provides a smooth transition from teacher-directed activities to SLP-led activities, builds rapport between teachers, students, and SLPs, and helps the SLP become more a part of the classroom. Small group and individual sessions can be used to more specifically target individual needs.

Special Considerations

Physical Impairments: For students with physical impairments, we must keep materials portable so that they are easily accessible. Instead of requiring children to come up to the board, for example, we can use a small board that goes to the student.

Visual Impairments: For students with visual impairments, we suggest a variety of auditory clips or tactile objects that go with each lesson.

Auditory Impairments: For students with auditory impairments, we have supplemented our instruction with a variety of visual aids and also suggest specific signs to target.

Augmentative Communication: For students with AAC devices, we suggest templates ranging in size from individual switches to large tablet-sized boards that can be used to program a wide variety of devices for the lessons.

Behavioral Concerns: For students with significant behavioral concerns we suggest ways to use scaled-down versions of materials typically used with a group. This allows the student to have ownership of his materials. Through our clinical research we have seen that students' undesired behaviors are often eliminated when they have a sense of responsibility and a clear purpose.

Create Routines

Consistent routines are a critical part of working with high needs students because they help reduce the cognitive demands, thereby freeing greater capacity for learning (Leinhardt, Weidman, & Hammond, 1987). Developing a routine is essential for allowing students to understand what is expected and what is coming next. Creating routines provides multiple opportunities for repetition of specific speech and language targets, as well as generalization between different themes. An additional benefit of consistent routines is that when children know what is coming next, they have a lower level of anxiety and are better prepared to learn (Jensen, 2009). Each lesson in these units follows the same basic structure for routines and activities. This allows students to learn the routine well, thereby maximizing their opportunities to learn.

Each lesson begins with a suggestion for objects to be used to work on pre-linguistic skills that tie in with the content covered in that specific lesson. For example, if we are doing a lesson that focuses on body parts, we can focus on joint attention goals within the context of the academic topic. A lesson on body parts could incorporate a puzzle activity in which you tap a puzzle piece and bring the child's attention to the "part" to be inserted into the "whole." Record the amount of support that is needed to have the child successfully take and place the piece. Individual attention and joint attention are critical for communication. Here are easy-to-follow protocols and citations for more information.

Initiate Joint Attention

The protocol for initiating joint attention requires that students perform each level for three days in a row (Whalen and Schreibman, 2003).

1. Initiating a point
2. Following eye gaze of communication partner

Use a Joint Attention Protocol

Whalen and Schriebman (2003) proposed protocols for training children to engage in and initiate joint attention. They suggest that at each level of the joint attention protocol, students should take the object of interest and engage with it for at least five seconds, five times in a row, for three consecutive days prior to moving to the next level. The protocols for engaging in joint attention and initiating joint attention, which are usually implemented in individual sessions, follow.

1. Response to being handed an object

2. Response to tapping on an object

3. Response to pointing to an object at a very close distance

4. Response to pointing to an object from at least 3 feet away

5. Response to pointing to an object at 8 feet away

Use Preference Assessments

Some students may require discrete trial training or behavioral strategies to learn new communication skills. Using the most effective reinforcers will increase a person's motivation to work for those reinforcers (Cuomo, 2012). Preference assessments are systematic ways of determining what items may act as reinforcers. There are many different types of preference assessments; however, we have included two methods below.

Item	Time
rocking horse	3 s
princess book	15 s
rocking horse	0 s
Barbie	10 s
princess book	15 s
Barbie	5 s

A single-item preference assessment is recommended for ranking objects or activities in order of preference. Present one object at a time and record how long the student engages with the item. Present all items in random order until all options have been presented. A sample data collection will look like the example to the right.

Pairing	Selected
chip and cheese	cheese
cracker and chip	cracker
cheese and cracker	cheese

A pair-wise preference assessment is recommended for ranking edible reinforcers in order of preference. To conduct a pair-wise assessment, present two food items at one time. When the student chooses their preferred item from the choice of two, remove the other item and present two new choices. Continue to present two choices until all items have been paired.

Assess Prior Knowledge

The purpose of the assessment of prior knowledge is to help students link information they already know about the topic to the discussion in the classroom (Whitehurst & Lonigan, 2003). An example of a question to probe prior knowledge could be, "Does anyone know of any animals that can be pets?" This gives the students an opportunity to answer open-ended questions. Then, scaffolding techniques can be used to help students make connections between the concept being taught and their personal experiences. Our goal is to engage students and check for understanding. Examples of different scaffolding techniques are described below.

Expand Communication using Scaffolding Techniques

Print reference - The adult references a target from the book by pointing or commenting (e.g. The adult points to an illustration and asks, "What is happening in the picture?").

Cloze procedures - The adult provides the first part of an utterance and the student completes the thought (e.g. A: The mouse lost his balance *and* _____ S: fell off).

Syntactic and semantic expansions—The adult expands on an utterance provided by the student using the grammar and vocabulary targets (e.g. S: The mouse walking. A: Yes, the little mouse is walking on the vine.).

Comprehension questions - The adult asks the student a question targeting an appropriate level of complexity for the student (A: Why do you think it could have been worse for the mouse? S: Because the cat could have eaten him).

Binary choice - The adult offers the student two choices of responses (e.g. A: What happened to the mouse? Did he fall off or jump off the vine? S: He fell off the vine.).

Modeling - The adult models the target structure for the student (e.g. What happened to the mouse when he was crossing the river? The mouse fell into the river.) (Liboiron & Soto, 2006).

UNIT COMPONENTS

Each unit begins with an information page that highlights specific language targets, the curriculum skills addressed, and a list of songs and materials needed to carryout the activities. The information page is a resource that can be shared with the classroom teacher to enhance collaboration. A modifications page is also included at the beginning of each unit. The modifications page allows the SLP and teacher to plan for diverse student needs within each lesson. Each unit also includes picture cards that can be used during the surprise bag activity, a sentence strip, visuals for a related song, games, a craft activity, and a recipe.

Each lesson plan highlights the suggested sound targets, a question of the day, a story, a story board, and comprehension questions. Below you will see a typical lesson plan structure incorporating all of the components mentioned previously. The first three activities are suggested to be done in a group. This is ideal when teachers and/or teacher aides are able to participate. For the following activities, it is optional to split the class into individual therapy sessions and/or small groups depending on students' needs. The lesson plan at the beginning of each unit provides an estimated time frame for each activity so you can select an activity or set of activities that will work within your time frame.

LESSON PLAN COMPONENTS

1. Question of the Day

2. Surprise Bag

3. Song

4. Discrete Trial Training (for joint attention or specific communication skills)

5. Articulation Chart

6. Story

7. Comprehension Questions

8. Game

> Note: All activities can be implemented individually or in small groups if they are not appropriate for all students .

9. Craft

10. Recipe

Question of the Day *(10-15 minutes)*

 This activity should be completed the same way for every lesson to increase the students' familiarity with the routine. The question of the day (QoD) is used to introduce the main topic of the lesson. The prompts used during the question of the day activity will vary based on the individual goals of the students. The QoD is usually a closed question, for which the instructor provides two or three choices of possible responses. It can be structured to allow students with different communication abilities to respond in a way that they can be successful. For example, if we were going to introduce the concept of pets, we would say, "Today we are going to talk about pets. Pets are animals that we take care of and they live in our home. The question of the day is, *What is your favorite pet?*" Underneath the question, we would present possible answers; a picture of a dog, a picture of a cat, and a blank card. Children would have the opportunity to answer non-verbally by placing their name under a picture choice, verbally by labeling the card of their choice after putting their name under it, or verbally by providing their own answer and placing their name under the black card. Responses can be targeted as imitations, single words, phrases, or complete sentences, depending on each student's communication level.

Materials: (1) Pictures and/or written names of each student

(2) Board

Prompts to get to QoD SLP Dialogue	Students' Dialogue	Targeted Goal
Whose picture/name is this?	*David!*	'Who' questions, literacy
Where is David?	*Next to Anna*	'Where' questions
What sound does "David" start with?	*/d/*	Phonological awareness
Let's clap out the syllables	*Da—vid*	Phonological awareness
Hi David, how are you?	*Fine, thanks* (shakes hand)	Greetings
Are you a girl or a boy?	"Boy" or "I am a boy." (sticks name under Boy as a non verbal answer)	Personal information
How many boys/girls are in your class?	3 boys, 1 girl	Quantitative concepts,
Are there more boys or more girls?	More boys	Plurals

Articulation Chart *(can be used in place of surprise bag activity)*

The articulation chart is a list of words that are part of the story in the lesson. They can be used for students to practice articulation skills in conjunction with language skills. The words are separated by target sounds. Students who are working on specific sounds may require individual therapy to have more repetitive practice producing target sounds, or the speech therapist may use the target words to plan ahead and provide students an opportunity for practice within the context of a group lesson. Here is an example of an articulation chart that is pre-filled with related vocabulary words that target specific sounds.

English

M   many, animals, jumping, climbing

N   many, animals, drinking, snake, end

B   bird, bee, buzzing, bear, rabbit

K   sky, squirrel, drinking, fox, walk, snake, climbing

G   grass, egg

T   water, eating, went, forest, rabbit, tree

D   bird, drinking, deer, end

F   forest, for, fox, flying

S   saw, forest, sky, squirrel, snake, slithering, sleeping

Surprise Bag *(10-15 minutes)*

The purpose of this activity is to introduce vocabulary used in the lesson. Have all of the students sit in a circle and take turns closing their eyes and pulling items out of the surprise bag. Surprise items vary according to the theme. Each chapter includes picture cards that may be printed and cut apart for quick lesson preparation. There are also suggestions for real objects to be used with each theme in the modifications table.

The following is a sample script.

SLP Dialogue	Students' Dialogue	Targeted Goal
Close your eyes, put your hand in, and pull out a surprise.	(Pulls out a surprise)	3-step directions
Whose turn is it?	*My turn/David's turn*	Requesting, turn-taking, 'who' questions
What would you like?	*I want to grab a surprise*	Requesting, sentence expansion
What do you have?	*A fish*	Labeling
What can a fish do?	*Swim*	Object function
Please put the fish on the board	(Puts the fish on the board)	1-step directions

During this activity, students can use prior knowledge to predict what they will find in the surprise bag. This will allow them to demonstrate their knowledge of semantic relationships such as categories, parts of a whole, and object functions. The activity also serves to increase vocabulary by building knowledge of concepts.

Game *(10-15 minutes)*

Games are an interactive way for students to get exposure to theme-based vocabulary. Included in each unit is a printable matching or bingo game. You can also create a game of 'fishing' by tying a magnet on the end of a string that is attached to a stick and using it to pick up vocabulary cards that are attached to paperclips. In addition to targeting speech and language goals, games are a "real world" way to teach appropriate pragmatic skills (i.e. turn-taking, establishing eye-contact, etc.).

Story book *(10-15 minutes)*

Each unit includes two stories. These stories can be read to a large group or a small group depending on the students' attentional, behavioral, and cognitive abilities. A **story board is also included as an accompaniment to each story. Story boards can be used to increase attention during story reading and also to** encourage participation for students who are nonverbal. *Story boards* can also be used to help students increase their mean length of utterance and/or improve syntactic structures (Bolderson, Dosanjh, Milligan, Pring, & Chiat, 2011).

While reading the book, use scaffolding techniques to engage the student and check understanding. Clinicians commonly use scaffolding techniques in order to help students learn target skills. Specific scaffolding techniques are presented in the story-reading section. They are effective during pre- and post-reading activities as well.

Comprehension Questions *(5-10 minutes)*

How can we assess comprehension? We ask questions. Each lesson includes suggested questions complete with visual modifications to be asked after each story. This allows us to use the visuals to assess a student's receptive language skills. You may also choose not to include visuals so that students are less likely to answer non-verbally. This allows for assessment of expressive language skills, such as the ability to formulate phrases or sentences appropriately, in addition to receptive language skills. Again, we have intentionally provided materials that can be manipulated to meet the student's individual needs and allow speech therapists to target a number of communicative goals.

While sitting at a table in a small group, students can complete a worksheet with questions about the story recently read. There are worksheets with multiple choice answers and worksheets that are open-ended. These worksheets are modified to meet the students' linguistic needs. Use language scaffolding techniques to enhance language skills when reviewing the answers to the questions. Allow students who have mastered a task to demonstrate the task for their classmates.

Crafts *(15-20 minutes)*

Crafts are beneficial for students who respond best to tactile input. Gather the materials listed at the beginning of each unit and make the minimal preparations. Empower and challenge students by having them set up for the activity. Explain what the students will be doing, show an example of the finished product and ask for helpers to gather colors, paper, glue, etc. Increase the level of difficulty by including a sequence of steps to follow, quantitative concepts or descriptions of the materials. Students can practice requesting materials, following directions, sequencing, and discussing what they did using past tense verbs.

Ask the initial helpers to gather and return the materials after completing the craft. Have students stand, present their work, comment or describe their work, and carry it to their backpack, folder, or cubbie.

Song *(5 minutes)*

Music supports the development of children's language skills because it encourages movement and repetition (Paquette & Rieg, 2008). The song activity can be done in a large group setting. This activity is great for breaking up seated activities and re-energizing the students. Provide visuals and allow students to pick the song. After students pick a song, place the song visual on a board. If there is time for more than one song, place both pictures on the board under the titles "first/then" or "primero/después." If the group of students requires more repetition, the same song can be sung for every lesson. Songs about greetings, days of the week, or songs that have gestures are great choices. Encourage participation with hand movements and the use of visuals.

Most of the vocabulary used in these songs has been pre-taught in the surprise bag activity so students have had an opportunity to become familiar with the words in the song. Pre-teaching vocabulary is important for increased participation (singing) while the song is playing. Each lesson also includes visuals to accompany the songs as a way to cue students while singing. Most of the song melodies are quick and easy to follow. When singing songs with your group, we recommend using the pause button frequently to allow students the opportunity to follow along. This is also a great strategy for eliciting language. Consider using the cloze procedure. For example, "Old MacDonald had (PAUSE)," and students respond, "A farm!" Then the music continues until the next pause.

Each lesson has a recommended song with printable visuals to use before, during, and/or after singing.

Materials: music player, song, printable visuals

Recipe *(20-25 minutes)*

 Each unit includes a printable recipe. The steps of the recipe are sequenced with pictures and words to help students request materials, describe what they are doing and review how they created the end product. The recipe activity is an extremely functional, "real world" application of the curriculum. Students can target multiple communication goals during this activity. More active students who benefit from hands-on activities may enjoy the freedom to move around while still engaging with the group and completing a specific task.

All of the activities in our lesson plans reinforce the topic of each unit through the use of games, crafts, or recipes. Many students who are not able to participate during story-time may be able to re-join the group and participate in more kinesthetic activities that allow them to move about the room. The games that we play can involve the picture cards used during the surprise bag activity. We can play a matching game in which students are expected to find pairs of picture cards. This allows them the opportunity to learn language concepts, such as same and different. It allows them the opportunity to practice naming or formulating sentences. It also enforces pragmatic skills such as waiting, turn-taking, winning or losing graciously, congratulating another and/or accepting congratulations graciously. Similarly, the craft and recipe activities can be used to target a variety of goals while allowing students to be successful in completing a functional daily living task.

Note: To condense the lesson plan, choose either a game, craft or recipe to use for the lesson plan that day. The same lesson plan can be used several times (by teachers and other professionals) using a different activity for each day.

HOW TO USE LIFE SKILLS LESSON PLANS IN YOUR CLASSROOMS

We have had great success using the following structure in theme-based units with our students in life skills classrooms and we know you will too.

These units were designed to be used in a classroom setting rather than in isolation. Get the teachers involved! Teachers and teacher assistants should be a part of these lessons as well. They may assist with providing cues, collecting data, or simply following along with the rest of the students. This will give everyone an opportunity to collaborate and discuss such things as ways to more appropriately modify for a particular student, ways to carry over information into other academic areas, ways to generalize skills being learned in speech therapy to other parts of the day, or progress to report to parents. It is a great way to build a collaborative team to support students in the life skills classroom.

Getting Started

We will start with the five basic steps and then cover each step in more detail.

1. Find out the teacher's schedule and discuss leading one or two portions of his or her class each week. Explain the purpose of aligning therapy plans with the curriculum.

2. Ask the teacher what themes he/she is currently focusing on.

3. Identify goals of each student and modify the activities using the modifications table.

4. Create a basic lesson plan to fit the length of your session using a lesson plan template.

5. Create a visual schedule to aid in organizing your sessions.

Preparation for Each Lesson Plan

1. Decide when to work with the students and whether the students will be seen in groups or individually.

Throughout the academic day teachers and speech-language pathologists can provide their students with many opportunities to communicate. For support personnel, such as speech-language pathologists, getting to know when the teacher and student have difficulty communicating can create a great opportunity to get buy-in. For example, if eating time is difficult, we can help the student to make choices. This leads to mastering communication goals and reducing the level of frustration in the classroom. Additionally, knowing a teacher's schedule allows us greater opportunities to have them participate in group activities that we have designed for their students. It can also provide an opportunity for assistance with individual goals that they would like their students to achieve.

2. Identify the current curriculum-based theme

By aligning our intervention and activities with the general education curriculum we can increase student communication, support the efforts of other professionals who work with these students, and reduce planning time.

Students progress when they have multiple opportunities to practice communicating about a single topic. When academic content and speech therapy are aligned, the student is using the same vocabulary and grammatical structures over and over. When the parents receive homework or information on the theme, this offers another opportunity to practice.

General education themes often come with materials and manipulatives that are related to the topic. By choosing the same theme, we reduce our planning time because the teacher may already have activities that we can support, may have manipulatives and objects that relate to the theme, and may have modifications such as augmentative communication set up in advance.

3. Identify goals and modify activities

Our students often have multiple disabilities and use communication devices or signing as a form of communication. By creating a modifications page we can easily physically modify materials to allow students with physical and behavioral challenges to participate linguistically. These modified materials target various levels of nonverbal to verbal communication. Each lesson contains modification suggestions related to the theme, and the following page shows how to modify your own materials.

4. Create a Lesson Plan

By creating a lesson plan you can organize your teaching around one academic topic and have activities planned for several sessions or weeks. Each unit contains two lesson plans. This section contains an example and blank templates for you to modify for your own activities. If possible, we suggest that you meet with others who work in the life skills classroom and make the materials together. Many professionals have cut their planning time in half by creating materials for multiple campuses at the same time. After you have created your lesson plan structure, minimal preparation time is needed for each plan.

Steps to begin

- Make a copy of the lesson plan template for each lesson and fill it in with the book, song and creative activities that you choose. List goals you will target for each activity. Refer to the sample lesson plan.

- Prepare the lesson by making copies of activity pages and homework sheets.

- Collect materials if applicable.

- Have audio files ready for the song and prepare auditory clips needed for any of the activities.

Routines

Each unit contains two lesson plans that can be divided in 15-minute increments depending on the schedules of the students. Each lesson contains the following routine:

1. Question of the Day

2. An articulation page that breaks vocabulary words up by syllables and sounds

3. Surprise Bag

4. Listening/Music Activity

5. Story-Based Lesson

6. Comprehension Questions

7. Creative Activities

8. Wrap-up

Modifying Intervention

Planning ahead is essential when working with children with profound disabilities. In order to access the curriculum, activities may need to be modified to take into account physical, emotional, or communication impairments. The modifications page of each lesson provides suggestions for modifying intervention for students with a variety of physical and behavioral impairments, as well as ways to modify for varying levels of communication.

Each lesson has a modifications table that is pre-filled with suggestions for many common impairments. By making changes to how the material is accessed, we allow the student to be successful while retaining the core knowledge that is the focus of the lesson. The *Community Workers* example on the following page demonstrates how this can be achieved. Also, use a blank table to create your own modifications table if you are planning to implement your own lessons with groups or individual students.

CONSIDERATION	MODIFICATION
Physical Impairments	
AAC Devices	
Visual Impairment	
Hearing Impairment	
Behavior	

Modification Example: Community Workers

Materials are made or gathered around a topic such as *community*. They vary in size, wording, and texture to accommodate different limitations. Here are suggestions for modifying the activity for different physical or intellectual limitations.

MODIFICATIONS

Physical Impairments	Felt board to reduce travel but increase participation with large group, family member cutouts on popsicle sticks, flashlight/light pointer
AAC Devices	Visuals and templates needed: peers, family members, places we go, switch visuals: *house, apartment, mom, dad*
Visual Impairment	Use objects from tactile schedule to symbolize places: *toy house, toy building (tall building for apartment), dolls/people, mom/dad*
Behavior	Behavior charts, visual schedules, and reward systems
Hearing Impairment	Signs: *mom, dad, school,* AAC device, pictures/visuals, sentence strips

COMMUNICATION ABILITIES

Nonverbal	Joint attention, use picture/word/sign to request preferred object/activity, identify peers/family members/self in pictures
Non Verbal + Gestures	Answer who/where questions by pointing to photos/objects
Low Verbal- 1 Word	Produce CV, VCV, CVCV combinations, label objects: *places and people in the community*, produce 3-syllable words: *family, hospital, lemonade library*
Verbal	Answer basic wh- questions, target prepositions, pronouns, and expand utterances

Lesson Plan Template Example

Theme: __All About Me!__   Date:_11/02/22_

Below is an example of a 90-minute speech therapy lesson plan. Modify this lesson plan as needed to fit your individual needs, including time in the classroom, student services recommended in the educational plan, and student goals.

Time	Schedule	Activity	Goals
15 min.	Discrete Trials	Individual time is recommended for students who: A. are working on pre-linguistic communication skills B. have significant behavioral challenges C. are working on very specific targets	Joint attention skills Identifying objects Turn-taking Articulation
15 min.	Question of the Day (QoD)	Name recognition: Clinician holds up name card and students identify their peer. Clap syllables of each name and focus on initial sounds. Clinician: **Whose name is on the card?** Students: **Jacob!** Clinician: **Where is Jacob?** Students: **Over there** Clinician: **That's right, he is next to Keith.** **Jacob, are you a boy or a girl?** Student: **I am a boy.** (Places his name under his answer) Clinician: **Let's look at everyone's answers. How many boys are in the class? How many girls are in the class? Are there more boys or more girls?** Students: **There are more boys.**	Phoneme identification Syllables Answering questions Joint attention Spatial concepts SVO sentences Quantitative concepts
5 min.	Language Goal	Clinician: **Today we are going to learn about _____.** Clinician: **What do we know about _____?** Assess prior knowledge.	1. Label: _____ 2. Verb: _____ 3. Target questions: _____

Lesson Plan Template (pg. 1 of 2)

Theme: _____   Date:_____

Below is an example of a 90-minute speech therapy lesson plan. Modify this lesson plan as needed to fit your individual needs, including time in the classroom, student services recommended in the educational plan, and student goals.

Time	Schedule	Activity	Goals
15 min.	Discrete Trials	Individual time is recommended for students who A. are working on pre-linguistic communication skills B. have significant behavioral challenges	Joint attention skills Identifying objects Turn-taking Articulation
15 min.	Question of the Day (QoD)	Clinician selects a QoD. Students respond verbal or non-verbally by selecting pictures. Clinician reviews the students' responses with the group.	Phoneme identification Syllables Answering questions Joint attention Spatial concepts SVO sentences Quantitative concepts
5 min.	Language Goal	Clinician: ***Today we are going to learn about _____.*** Clinician: ***What do we know about _____?*** Assess prior knowledge.	1. Label: _____ 2. Verb: _____ 3. Target questions: _____

Lesson Plan Template (pg. 2 of 2)

Theme: _____   Date: _____

Time	Schedule	Activity	Goals
15 min.	Surprise Bag	Place _____ in a bag. Clinician: **Today we are talking about _____. What do you think is in the bag?** Pass the bag around and use the same sequence instructions for each student. **Close your eyes. Put your hand in the bag. Take out your surprise.** Clinician: **What do you have?** Student: _____ Clinician: **Yes it is a _____. (follow up question)**	Naming/labeling _____ Following directions
5 min.	Song	Introduce the name of the song and vocabulary in the song. Have the students dance with the song, pairing gestures with key concepts.	Expanding utterances: "I want + to sing + _____"
15 min.	Story	Read the book _____ Use scaffolding techniques and the story board while reading the book.	Label _____ Answering questions SVO sentence structures
15 min.	Comprehension Questions	Students complete the worksheets to "test" what they have learned from the story. Provide worksheets with multiple choice modifications for students who need scaffolding support.	Answering questions Produce phrases/sentences Syntax (word order, obligatory words)
5 min.	Wrap Up and Clean Up	Review the overall main topic and specific language target and/or sound target that you focused on. **Today we learned about _____. We also talked about sounds we make _____.**	

5. Create a Visual Schedule

Creating a visual schedule enables the students to follow the progression of your session and enables you to plan effectively. With a little work at the beginning, you can create a schedule that can be reused throughout the year. We use the same icons across all of our units to symbolize the different types of activities, which cuts down on the amount of work we do and increases the students' familiarity and expectations for each activity.

How to make a visual schedule

Copy, cut out, and laminate the following page. You can make more visual schedules if you want each student to have his own schedule. Create a vertical or horizontal wall chart or a flip book. Mount Velcro on the back of each picture to be arranged on your visual schedule board. These pictures can also be used as icons in an augmentative communication device.

How to use a visual schedule

Choose the activities that you are going to do that day. Note: do not try to do everything on the schedule! A typical session has the same intro and wrap-up, and 2-3 activities in between.

Here are some excellent ways to adapt the visual schedule:

- Empower your students by letting *them* choose what they would like to do that day. After a while, students will develop favorites and they can choose one out of the two or three activities that you would like to plan for the following schedule.

- Use the visual schedule for initiation and completion. Before a student starts an activity they add it to the visual schedule. After a student finishes an activity, they remove the icon from the schedule. This teaches progress, motivates them to keep going, and lets them know that the end is in sight.

- Create a separate visual schedule for their classroom and have the teacher create icons that represent the activities that make up the rest of the student's day.

Visual Schedule Pictures

Cut out, laminate and put on a vertical strip or in a communication binder.

question of the day	surprise bag	song
pregunta del día	*bolsa de sorpresa*	*canción*
story	story questions	game
cuento	*preguntas del cuento*	*juego*
crafts	recipe	listen
	receta	*escuchar*
work	group	Individual
trabajo	*grupo*	*individual*

A color version of this visual schedule is available in the resource library at: www.bilinguistics.com.

Unit 4

Animals in Their Homes

Los animales y sus hogares

ANIMALS IN THEIR HOMES

Language Focus:

Identify and/or label animals and places.

Categorize animals based on where they live and/or by attributes.

Explain semantic relationships between objects.

Curriculum Skills by Grade:

K.   Examine evidence that living organisms have basic needs, such as food, water, and shelter for animals.

1.   Investigate how the external characteristics of an animal are related to where it lives, how it moves, and what it eats.

2.   Compare and give examples of the ways living organisms depend on each other and on their environments.

3.   Explore how structures and functions of animals allow them to survive in a particular environment.

4.   Explore how adaptations enable organisms to survive in their environment.

5.   Compare the structures and functions of different species that help them live and survive.

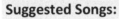

Suggested Songs:

English	Spanish
Five little monkeys– Juan Luis Orozco	Cinco monitos– Juan Luiz Orozco
Octopus– Charlotte Diamond	Un pulpito– Charlotte Diamond

Materials	Recipe Ingredients (*per student)
Paper plates	1 bottle of water
Scissors	2-3 drops of blue food coloring
Glue	1 tbs brown sugar
Crayons	1 Swedish fish, 1 gummy worm,
Popsicle sticks	1 gummy octopus, 1 gummy shark

Content

4

**ANIMALS IN
THEIR HOMES**

Section	Schedule	Activity	Goals
		Lesson 1 and 2	
4A	Surprise Bag	Animal pictures or plastic animals	• Follow directions • Identify animals receptively • Label animals • Formulate sentences • Target basic concepts (size,
4B	Song	1. The Octopus Song by Charlotte Diamond 2. Un pulpito by Charlotte Diamond	• Answer questions • Target quantitative concepts • Target vocabulary
4C	Sentence Strip	The _____ lives in the _____.	• Expand utterances • Target semantic relationships
4D	Question of the Day	1. Where do you live?/¿Dónde vives? 2. What is your favorite pet?/¿Cúal es tu mascota favorita?	• Expanding utterances • Answering questions

4E	Story	1. A Walk Through the Forest/Un paseo por el bosque
		
		    A. Story board
		
		2. Where can Paco live?/¿Dónde puede vivir Paco?
		
		    A. Story Board
			• Follow directions
			
			• Answer questions
			
			• Sequence
			
			• Expand utterances
			
			• Identify animals and their homes
			
			• Label vocabulary of animals and their homes
			
			• Target semantic relationships

Content

Section	Schedule	Activity	Goals
		Lesson 1 and 2	
4F	Story Questions	Low-tech picture boards Story question pages Icon sentence strips	• Answer questions • Expand utterances
4G	Story Articulation	Story vocabulary listed by sound	• Target articulation/ phonology
4H	Game	Matching game	• Follow directions • Target semantic relationships
4I	Crafts	Animal masks	• Follow directions • Answer questions • Sequence • Label • Expand utterances
4J	Recipe	Make ocean water	• Follow directions • Answer questions • Label • Expand utterances • Sequence

Lesson Plan 1 (pg. 1 of 2)

Date:_____

Below is an example of a 90-minute speech therapy lesson plan. Modify this lesson plan as needed to fit your individual needs, including time in the classroom, student services recommended in the educational plan, and student goals.

4

ANIMALS IN THEIR HOMES

Time	Schedule	Activity	Goals
15 min.	Discrete Trials	What do you like? - reinforcement test/preference assessment Joint attention protocol Suggested objects: Wind-up animals Identify self in picture Identify teacher in picture	Increase joint attention skills Identification of objects Take turns Practice articulation
15 min.	Question of the Day (QoD)	QoD: *"What animal do you like best"* Clinician: *Today, we are going to talk about animals and where they live.* Go around room and ask, *What is your favorite forest animal?* Provide a visual of bird, rabbit and blank card for additional answers. Clinician: *Can anyone think of other animals that live in the forest?* Ask a friend, *What animal do you like best?*	Identify phonemes Mark syllables Answer questions Increase joint attention skills Produce SVO sentences
5 min.	Language Goal	Clinician: *Today we are going to learn about animals in their homes.* Clinician: *What animals live in the forest?* Assess prior knowledge.	1. Label: animals 2. Describe the actions of animals 3. Answer questions

Date:_____

4

**ANIMALS IN
THEIR HOMES**

Time	Schedule	Activity	Goals
15 min.	Surprise bag	Place surprise bag cards in a bag. Clinician: ***Today we are talking about animals. What do you think is in the bag?*** Pass the bag around and use the same sequence instruction for each student. ***Close your eyes. Put your hand in the bag. Take out your surprise.*** Clinician: ***What do you have?*** Student: _____ Clinician: ***Yes it is a _____. (follow up question)***	Name/label objects Follow directions
5 min.	Song	Introduce the song "Slippery Fish (The Octopus Song)" and vocabulary in the song. Have the students dance with the song, pairing gestures and pictures with key concepts	Name/Label Expand utterances: "I want to sing + octopus"
15 min.	Story	Read the book *A Walk Through the Forest.* Use scaffolding techniques and the story board while reading the book	Label animals Answer questions SVO sentence structures
15 min.	Comprehension Questions	Students complete the worksheets to "test" what they have learned from the story. Provide worksheets with multiple choice modifications for students who need scaffolding support.	Answer questions Produce phrases/sentences Use correct syntax (word order, obligatory words)
5 min.	Wrap-Up and Clean Up	Review the language target and/or sound target. ***Today we learned about animals, what they do, and where they live. We also talked about sounds we make.***	

Lesson Plan 2 (pg. 1 of 2)

Date:_____

Below is an example of a 90-minute speech therapy lesson plan. Modify this lesson plan as needed to fit your individual needs, including time in the classroom, student services recommended in the educational plan, and student goals.

4

ANIMALS IN THEIR HOMES

Time	Schedule	Activity	Goals
15 min.	Discrete Trials	Preference assessment Joint attention protocol Objects: stuffed animals, wind up animals	Develop joint attention skills Identify objects Develop turn-taking skills Produce articulation targets
15 min.	Question of the Day (QoD)	QoD: *"What is your favorite pet?"* Provide visuals of a fish, dog, cat, and a black card for additional answers. Clinician, *"What is this animal like?" "What does it look like?" "Where does it live?"* Clinician, *"Is it big, small, long, short, furry, smooth?"*	Identify phonemes Produce all syllables Maintain joint attention Produce SVO sentences Answer questions
5 min.	Language goal	Clinician: *Today we are going to learn about animals in their homes.* Clinician: *Where do animals live?* Assess prior knowledge	Label: animals, homes Verbs: actions of animals Answer questions
15 min.	Surprise Bag	Place surprise bag cards in a bag. Clinician: *Today we are talking about body parts. What do you think is in the bag?* Pass the bag around and use the same sequence instruction for each student. *Close your eyes. Put your hand in the bag. Take out your surprise.* Clinician: *What do you have?* Student: _____ Clinician: *Yes it is a _____. (follow up question)*	Name body parts Follow directions

Date:_____

4

ANIMALS IN THEIR HOMES

Time	Schedule	Activity	Goals
5 min.	Song	Review the song 'The Octopus Song' and vocabulary in the song. Have the students dance with the song, pairing gestures with key concepts.	Name/Label Expand utterances: "I want + to sing + octopus"
15 min.	Story	Read the book *Where Can Paco Live?* Use scaffolding techniques and the story board while reading the book.	Label body parts Answer questions Produce SVO sentence structures
15 min.	Comprehension Questions	Students complete the worksheets to "test" what they have learned from the story. Provide worksheet with multiple choice modifications for students who need scaffolding support.	Answer questions Produce phrases/sentences Use correct syntax (i.e., word order, obligatory words)
5 min.	Wrap Up and clean Up	Review the language target and/or sound target. ***Today we learned about how we are the same and ways we are different. We also talked about sounds we make.***	

Modifications

Physical Impairments– Low Mobility	Modification: Felt/dry erase board for non-ambulatory students Template to match items in the surprise bag vs. pulling them out
AAC Devices	Visuals and Templates needed: 1) animals 2) habitats Switches- "Look out!" or "I see an animal."
Visual Impairment	Objects: Wind-up animals, boxes, tubes
Hearing Impairment	Signs: *in, out, common animals (dog/cat/fish/bird), walk, fly, swim* Visuals: see story boards and sentence strips
Behavior	Personal object/activity: Hide and seek

Communication Abilities

Nonverbal	Joint attention Use picture/word/sign to request preferred object/activity
Nonverbal + Gestures	Follow directions: *stop, go, go to (location)* Imitate- CV, VCV, CVCV combinations English: *my, go, out, take, car, bus, life, look, light, cow, house* Spanish: *mi, tu, el, la, alto, carro, bos, luz, mira, vida, vaca, casa*
Low Verbal- 1 Word	Produce- CV, VCV, CVCV combinations Label objects: *apartment, house, city, country, park, field, car, tractor, horse, cow, people, light* Target words: *stop, go*
Verbal	Expressive Goals: Increase MLU: prepositional phrases Sentence strip: "I like to (verb phrase) in the (location)."

Surprise Bag

camel	bird	bear
camello	*pájaro*	*oso*
rabbit	crab	fish
conejo	cangrejo	pez
octopus	squirrel	deer
pulpo	*ardilla*	venado
snake	frog	whale
víbora	*rana*	*ballena*

Song

4

ANIMALS IN THEIR HOMES

Song Activity: *5 Little Monkeys/Cinco monitos pequeños*

Suggested goals to target:

- Vocabulary: monkey, alligator, tree, swinging, snatched etc.

- Quantitative concepts: more, less, one, all, etc.

- Wh– questions: What happened? Who ate the monkey? How many? etc.

Purpose:

- Use attached visual cues.

- Teach concepts prior to the song, reinforce concepts during the song, and review concepts after the song.

- Identify and label targeted vocabulary when learning the song's lyrics.

- Ask and answer questions, such as, "Who ate the monkey?"

- Identify and/or label sequencing concepts, such as, "first/last."

- Encourage and facilitate participation in group activities.

- Increase and maintain attention to group activities.

Suggested activities:

- Review quantitative concepts

- Cut and place Velcro on pictures of monkeys and place them in the tree. Students take turns using the alligator to 'snatch' a monkey off of the tree. After each verse, ask the students, "What happened?" "Who snatched the monkey?" "How many monkeys are left?" etc.

Song Visuals

desert	forest	ocean
pond	bird	bear
camel	frog	octopus
squirrel	deer	whale
rabbit	crab	fish

English Sentence Strip

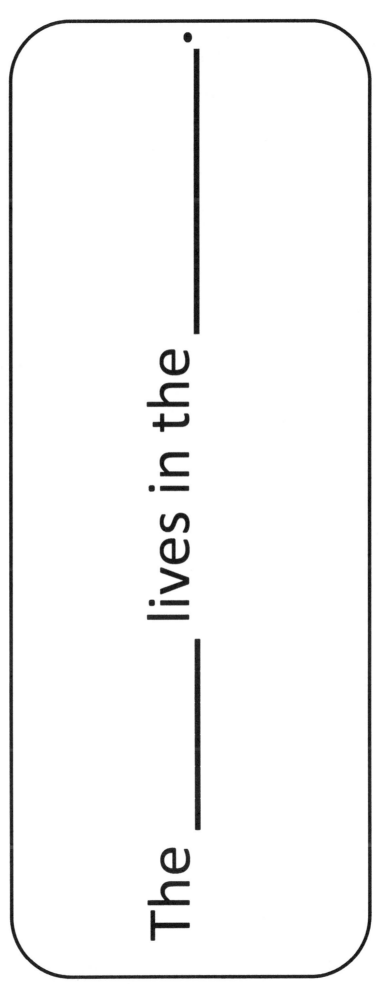

The _____ lives in the _____ .

49

desierto	bosque	océano
estanque	pájaro	oso
camello	rana	pulpo
ardilla	venado	ballena
conejo	cangrejo	pez

Spanish Sentence Strip

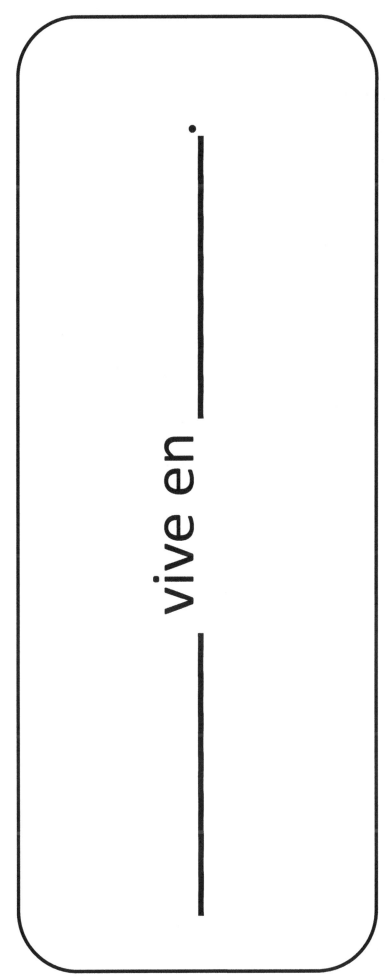

_____ vive en _____.

Question of the Day 1

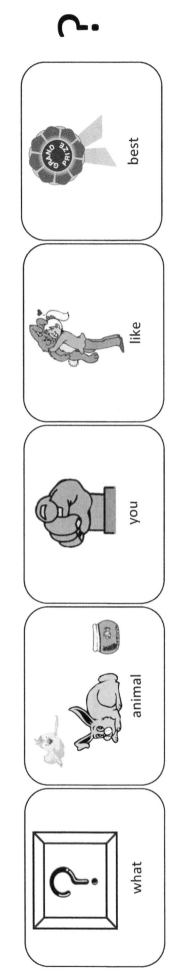

ANIMALS IN
THEIR HOMES

4

what

animal

you

like

best

?.

fish

rabbit

bird

*What animal do you like best?

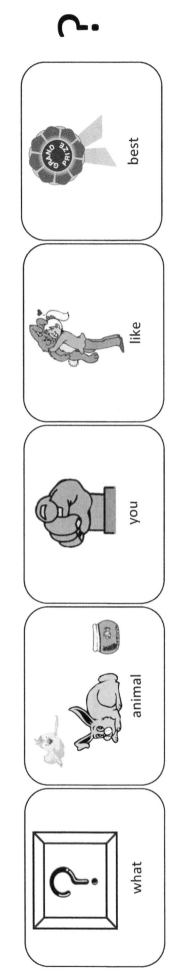

La pregunta del día 1

?.

favorito

tu

animal

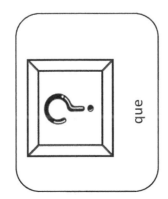

que

:?

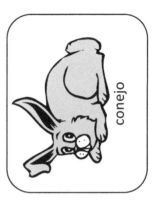

conejo

pez

pájaro

*Que animal es tu favorito?

Story 1 / Cuento 1

A Walk Through the Forest.

Un paseo por el bosque.

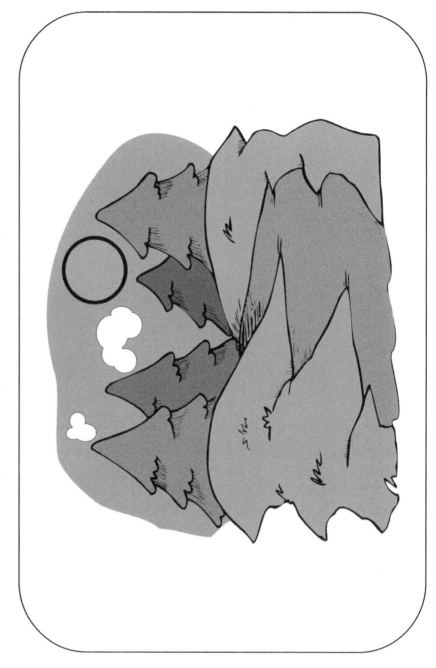

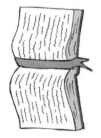

I went for a walk in the forest. Many animals live in the forest.

Caminé por el bosque. Muchos animales viven en el bosque.

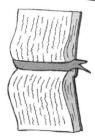

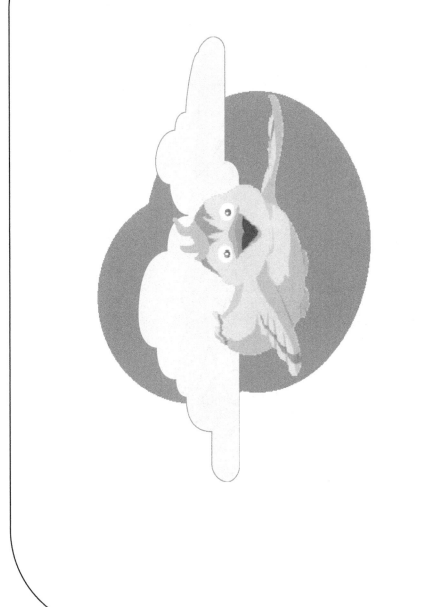

I saw a bird flying in the sky. The bird lives in the forest.

Vi un pájaro volando en el cielo. El pájaro vive en el bosque.

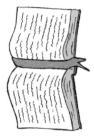

I saw a rabbit jumping. The rabbit lives in the forest.

Vi un conejo brincando. El conejo vive en el bosque.

I saw a squirrel climbing a tree. The squirrel lives in the forest.

Vi una ardilla trepando un árbol. La ardilla vive en el bosque.

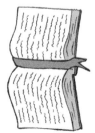

I saw a snake slithering in the grass. The snake lives in the forest.

Vi una serpiente arrastrándose en el pasto. La serpiente vive en el bosque.

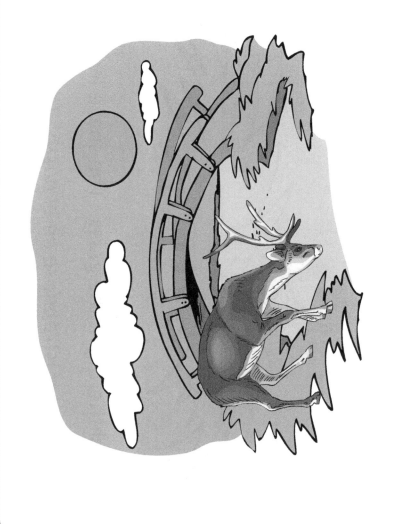

I saw a deer drinking water. The deer lives in the forest.

Vi un venado tomando agua. El venado vive en el bosque.

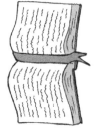

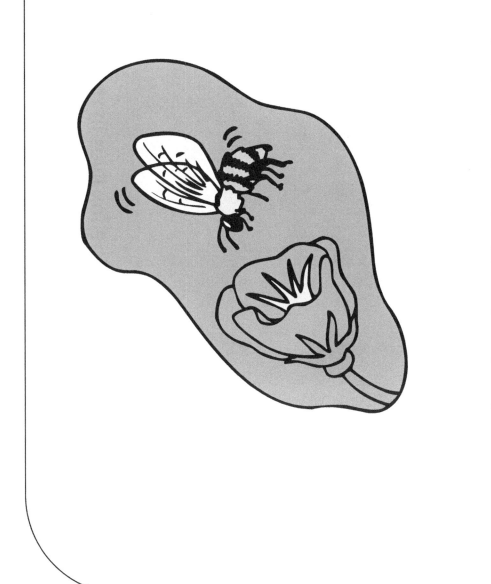

I saw a bee buzzing. The bee lives in the forest.

Vi una abeja zumbando. La abeja vive en el bosque.

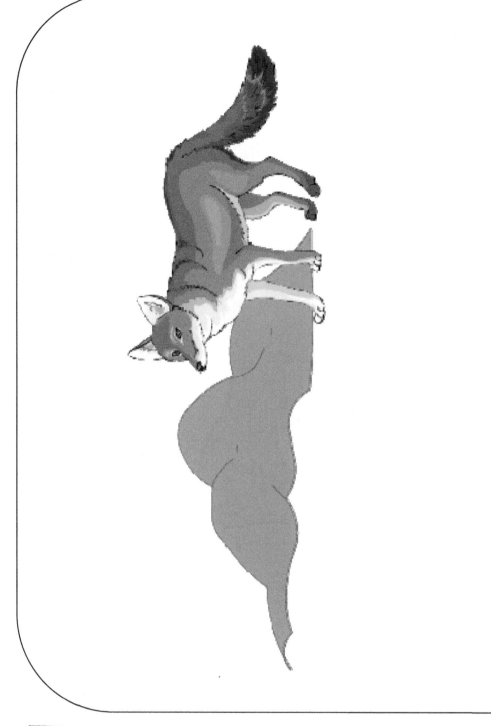

I saw a fox digging. The fox lives in the forest.

Vi un zorro escarbando. El zorro vive en el bosque.

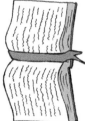

I saw an owl sleeping in a tree. The owl lives in the forest.

Vi un búho durmiendo en el árbol. El búho vive en el bosque.

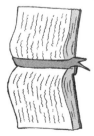

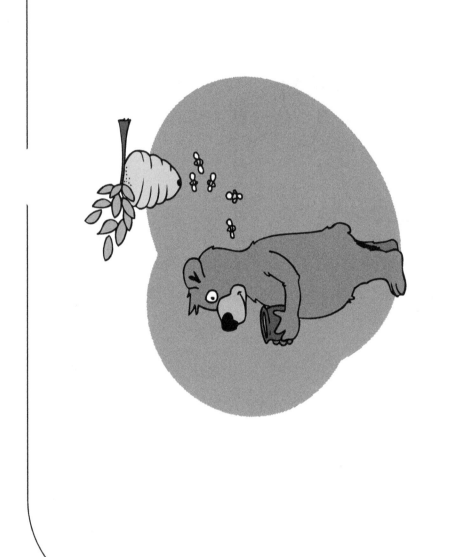

I saw a bear eating. The bear lives in the forest.

Vi un oso comiendo. El oso vive en el bosque.

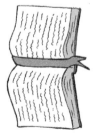

I saw many animals in the forest.

Vi muchos animales en el bosque.

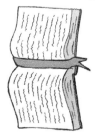

The End

El fin

A Walk Through the Forest

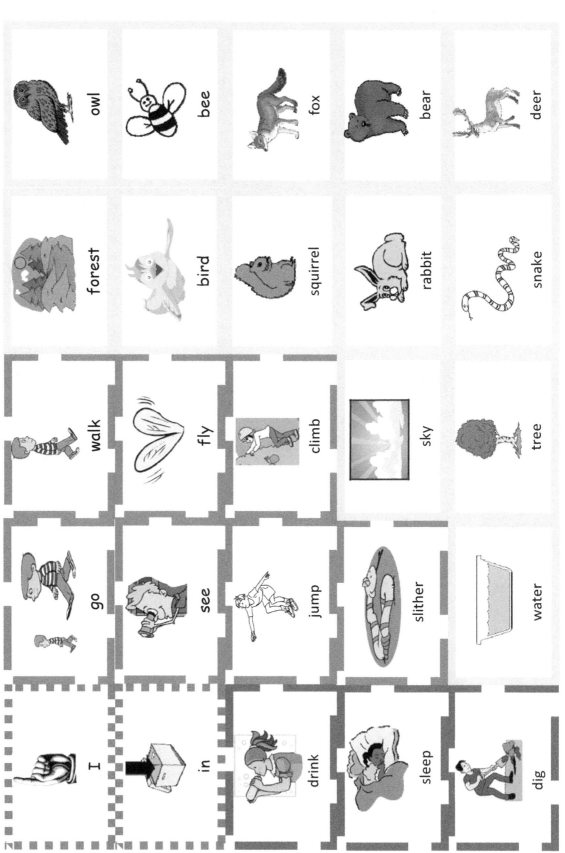

Un paseo por el bosque

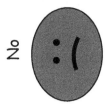

No

Sí

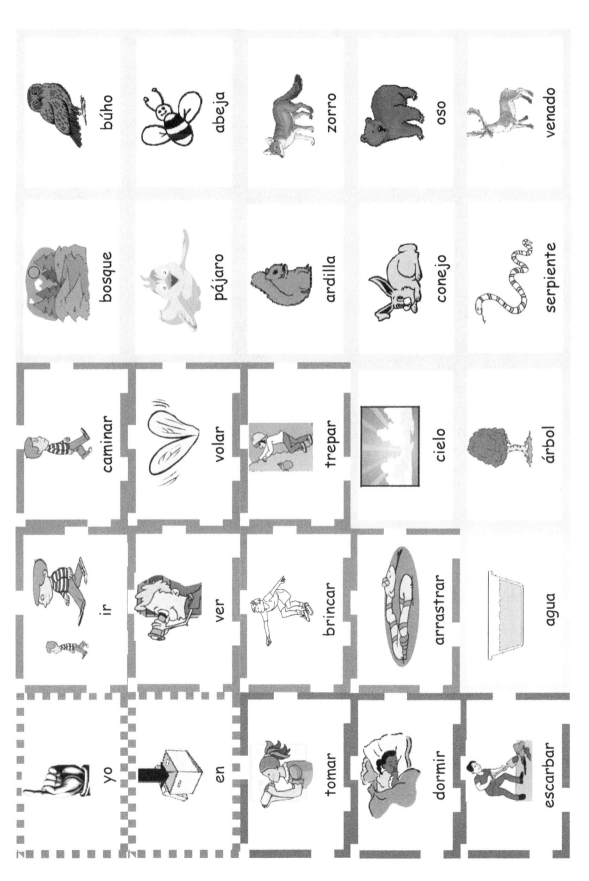

búho

abeja

zorro

oso

venado

bosque

pájaro

ardilla

conejo

serpiente

caminar

volar

trepar

cielo

árbol

ir

ver

brincar

arrastrar

agua

yo

en

tomar

dormir

escarbar

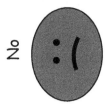

Story 1 Questions

1. What lives in the forest?

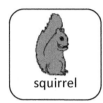
squirrel

cat

elephant

2. What does a rabbit do?

swim

jump

run

3. Where does the bear live?

desert

jungle

forest

4. What slithers in the grass?

bird

fox

snake

5. What animal buzzes?

kangaroo

bee

spider

Story 1 Questions

1. What lives in the forest?

2. What does a rabbit do?

3. Where does the bear live?

4. What slithers in the grass?

5. What animal buzzes?

 # Preguntas del cuento 1 **4**

1. ¿Qué vive en el bosque?

 ardilla

 gato

 elefante

2. ¿Qué hace un conejo?

 nadar

 brincar

 correr

3. ¿Dónde vive el oso?

 desierto

 selva

 bosque

4. ¿Qué se arrastra en el pasto?

 pájaro

 zorro

 culebra

5. ¿Cuál animal zumba?

 canguro

 abeja

 araña

Preguntas del cuento 1

1. ¿Qué vive en el bosque?

2. ¿Qué hace un conejo?

3. ¿Dónde vive el oso?

4. ¿Qué se arrastra en el pasto?

5. ¿Cuál animal zumba?

English Articulation Words

Story 1: A Walk Through the Forest.

4 ANIMALS IN THEIR HOMES

English

M **m**any, ani**m**als, ju**m**ping, cli**m**bing

N ma**n**y, a**n**imals, dri**n**king, s**n**ake, e**n**d

B **b**ird, **b**ee, **b**uzzing, **b**ear, ra**bb**it

K s**k**y, s**qu**irrel, drin**k**ing, fo**x**, wal**k**, sna**k**e, **c**limbing

G **g**rass, e**gg**

T wa**t**er, ea**t**ing, wen**t**, fores**t**, rabbi**t**, **t**ree

D bir**d**, **d**rinking, **d**eer, en**d**

F **f**orest, **f**or, **f**ox, **f**lying

S **s**aw, fore**s**t, **s**ky, **s**quirrel, **s**nake, **s**lithering, **s**leeping

L **l**ive, anima**l**s, f**l**ying, c**l**imbing, s**l**ithering, s**l**eeping, squirre**l**, ow**l**

R **r**abbit, fo**r**est, bi**r**d, squi**r**rel, t**r**ee, slithe**r**ing, g**r**ass, d**r**inking, fo**r**, dee**r**, bea**r**, th**r**ough

Sonidos del habla—Español

Cuento 1: *Un paseo por el bosque.*

4

ANIMALS IN
THEIR HOMES

Spanish

M	**m**uchos, ani**m**ales, ca**m**iné, to**m**ando, zu**m**bando, dur**m**iendo, co**m**iendo
P	**p**aseo, **p**or, **p**ájaro, **p**asto, tre**p**ando, ser**p**iente
B	**b**osque, **v**enado, **b**úho, ár**b**ol, a**b**eja, zum**b**ando, escar**b**ando, **b**rincando
K	**c**aminé, **c**onejo, **c**omiendo, bos**qu**e, brin**c**ando, escar**b**ando
N	cami**n**é, a**n**imales, vola**n**do, co**n**ejo, u**n**a, trepa**n**do, serpie**n**te, arrastra**n**do, ve**n**ado, toma**n**do, zumba**n**do, escarba**n**do, durmie**n**do, comie**n**do, u**n**, vive**n**, e**n**, bri**n**cando
T	**t**omando, serpien**t**e, arras**t**rando, pas**t**o, **t**repando
D	**d**urmien**do**, volan**do**, brincan**do**, trepan**do**, ar**d**illa, arrastran**do**, toman**do**, vena**do**, zumban**do**, escarban**do**, comien**do**
S	**c**ielo, **s**erpiente, **z**umbando, **z**orro, pa**s**eo, bo**s**que, arra**s**trando, pa**s**to, e**s**carbando, o**s**o, mucho**s**, animale**s**
L	anima**l**es, vo**l**ando, cie**l**o, e**l**, árbo**l**
R	escarband**o**, du**r**miendo, á**r**bol, pája**r**o, b**r**incando, t**r**epando, a**r**dilla, se**r**piente, a**rr**astrando, zo**rr**o, po**r**

La pregunta del día 2

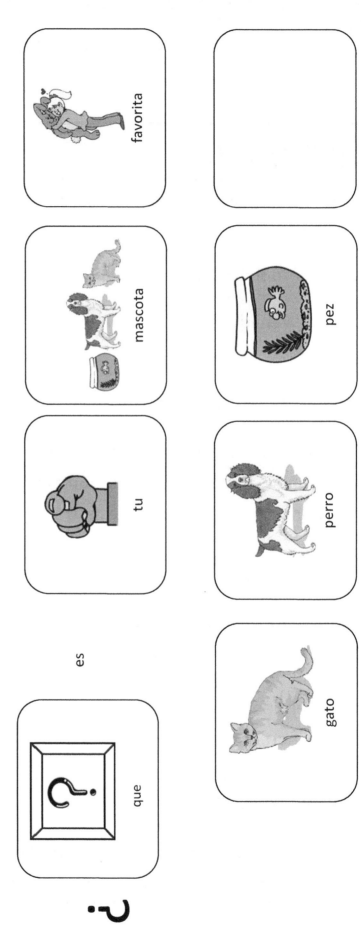

favorita

mascota

pez

tu

perro

es

que

gato

Question of the Day 2

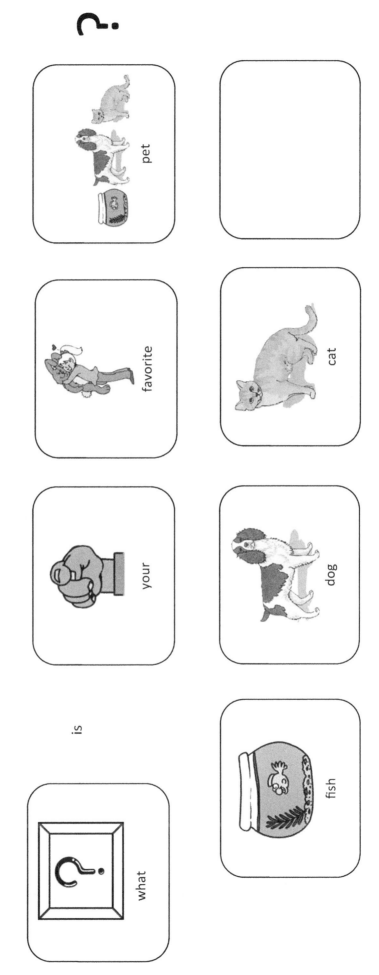

what

is

your

favorite

pet

dog

cat

fish

?

Story 2 / Cuento 2

Where can Paco live?

¿Dónde puede vivir Paco?

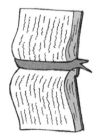

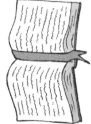

Paco needs a home. Where can he live?

Paco necesita un hogar. ¿Dónde puede vivir?

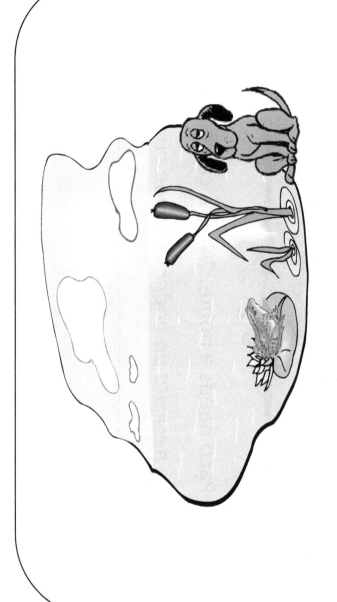

Can Paco live with the frog? No, the frog lives in the pond.

¿Puede vivir Paco con la rana? No, la rana vive en el estanque.

Can Paco live with the deer? No, the deer lives in the forest.

¿Puede vivir Paco con el venado? No, el venado vive en el bosque.

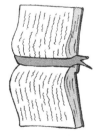

Can Paco live with the camel? No, the camel lives in the desert.

¿Puede vivir Paco con el camello? No, el camello vive en el desierto.

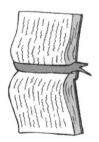

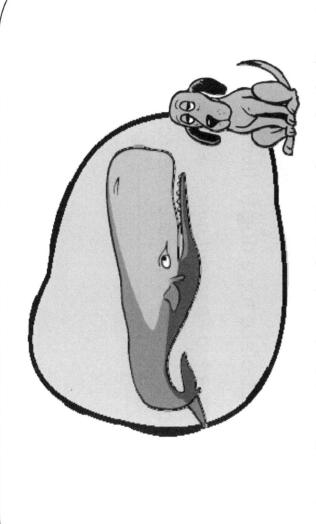

Can Paco live with the whale? No, the whale lives in

the ocean.

¿Puede vivir Paco con la ballena? No, la ballena vive

en el océano.

Can Paco live in the boy's house? Yes, a house is a perfect place for a dog to live!

¿Puede vivir Paco en la casa del niño? Sí, una casa es uh hogar perfecto para un perro.

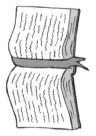

The End

El Fin

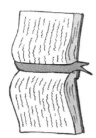

Where can Paco live?

 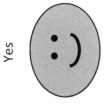

¿Dónde puede vivir Paco?

No

Sí
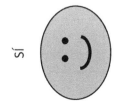

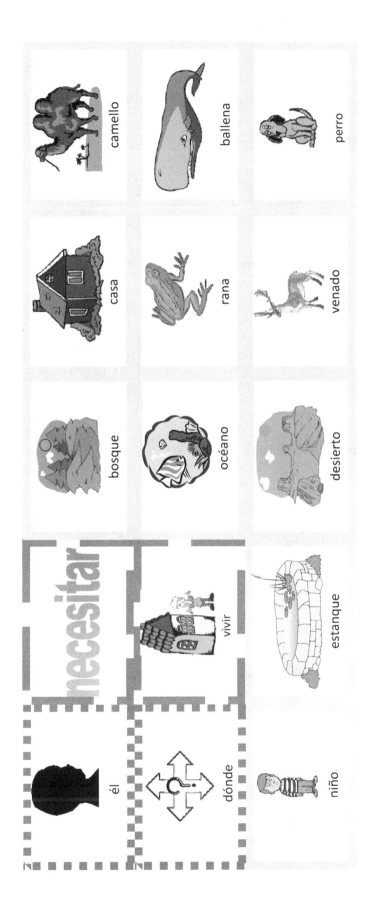

camello

ballena

perro

casa

rana

venado

bosque

océano

desierto

necesitar

vivir

estanque

él

dónde

niño

Story 2 Questions

1. Where does the deer live?

 forest
 building
 ocean

2. Where does the camel live?

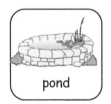 pond
 school
 desert

3. Where does the whale live?

 ocean
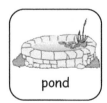 house
 park

4. Where does the frog live?

 school
 pond
 forest

5. Where does the boy live?

 ocean
 house
 desert

Story 2 Questions

1. Where does the deer live?

2. Where does the camel live?

3. Where does the whale live?

4. Where does the frog live?

5. Where does the boy live?

 # Preguntas del cuento 2 **4**

1. ¿Dónde vive el venado?

 bosque  edificio  océano

2. ¿Dónde vive el camello?

 estanque  escuela  desierto

3. ¿Dónde vive la ballena?

 océano  casa  parque

4. ¿Dónde vive la rana?

 escuela  estanque  bosque

5. ¿Dónde vive el niño?

 océano  casa  desierto

Preguntas del cuento 2

1. ¿Dónde vive el venado?

2. ¿Dónde vive el camello?

3. ¿Dónde vive la ballena?

4. ¿Dónde vive la rana?

5. ¿Dónde vive el niño?

English Articulation Words

Story 2: Where can Paco live?

English

M camel, home

N can, ocean, pond

P Paco, place, pond, perfect

K can, camel, Paco, perfect

G frog, dog

T forest, desert, perfect

D deer, desert, dog, pond

F forest, perfect, frog

S desert, house, place, forest

L live, camel, whale, place

R forest, perfect, where, deer, frog, desert

Sonidos del habla—Español

Cuento 2: *¿Dónde puede vivir Paco?*

4 ANIMALS IN THEIR HOMES

Spanish

M camello

P Paco, puede, perfecto, perro

B ballena, vivir, venado, bosque

K camello, casa, Paco, estanque, bosque, perfecto

N necesita, niño, rana, venado, ballena, océano, donde, estanque

T necesita, estanque, desierto, perfecto

D donde, desierto, puede, venado

S necesita, desierto, océano, casa, estanque, bosque

R rana, hogar, desierto, perfecto, vivir

Match Game Board

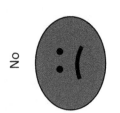

No

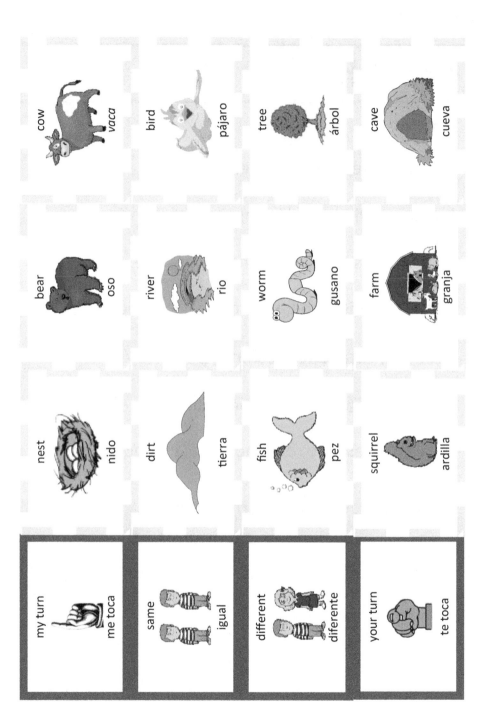

cow / *vaca*	bear / oso	nest / nido
bird / pájaro	river / rio	dirt / tierra
tree / árbol	worm / gusano	fish / pez
cave / cueva	farm / granja	squirrel / ardilla

my turn / me toca	same / igual
different / diferente	your turn / te toca

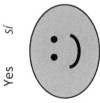

Yes   sí

Match Game Cards

nest	bear	cow
nido	*oso*	*vaca*
dirt	river	bird
tierra	*rio*	*pájaro*
fish	worm	tree
pez	*gusano*	*árbol*
squirrel	farm	cave
ardilla	*granja*	*cueva*

Craft Activity: Animal Masks

1. Choose — bear — cat — or — rabbit

2. Cut — ears — eyes — nose — and — mouth

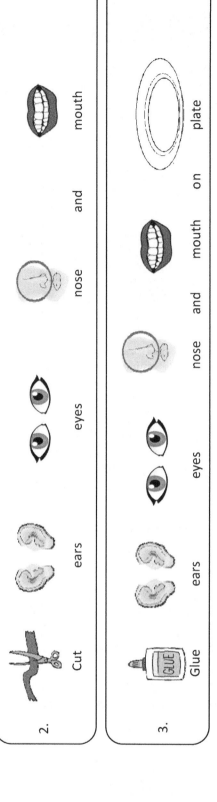

3. Glue — ears — eyes — nose — and — mouth — on — plate

4. Glue — popsicle stick — on back of — plate

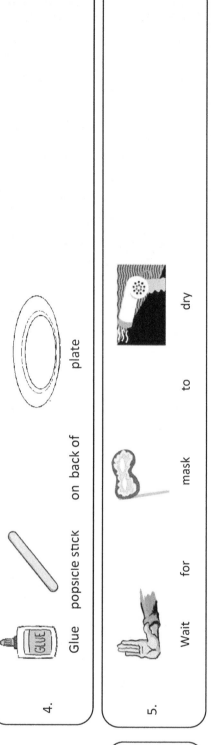

5. Wait — for — mask — to — dry

First

Last

Arte: Máscara de animal

1. Escoge — oso — gato — o — conejo

Primero

2. Cortar — orejas — ojos — nariz — boca

3. Pegar — orejas — ojos — nariz — y — boca — en — plato

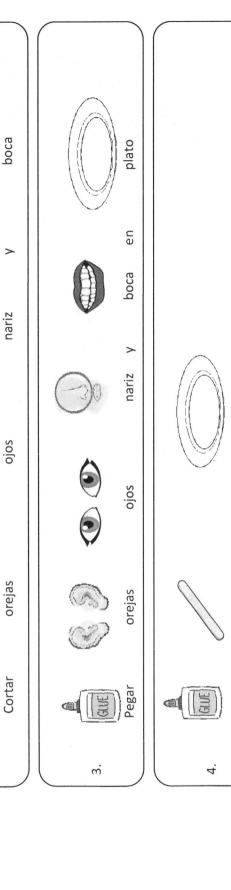

4. Pegar — palo — detrás — plato

5. Esperar — máscara — secar

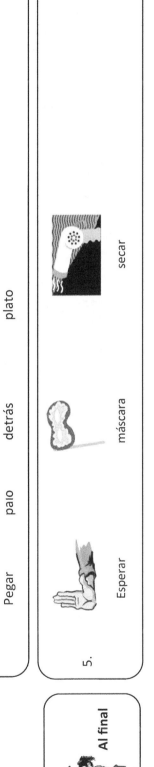

Al final

Craft Activity: Animal Ears

Rabbit

Bear

Cat

Craft Activity: Animal Eyes, Noses and Mouths

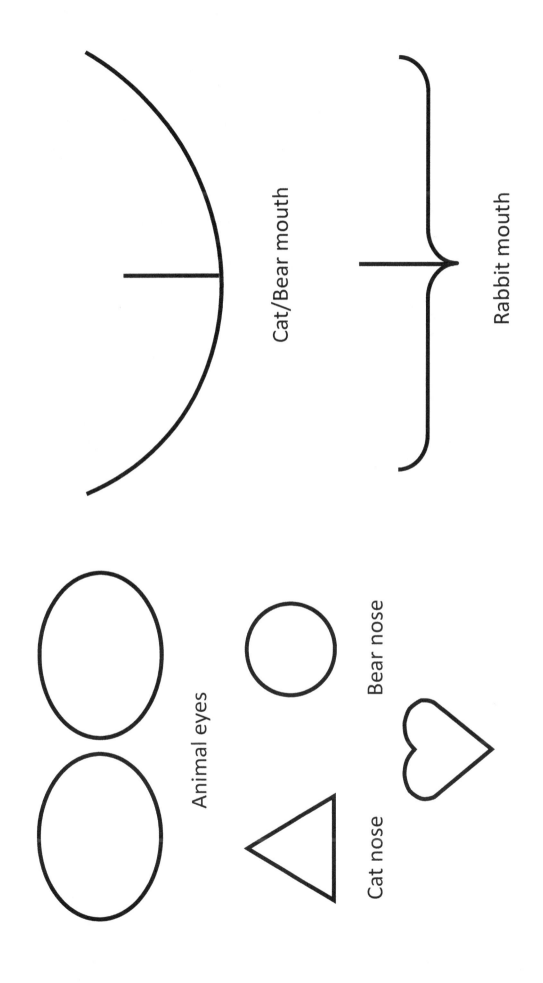

Animal eyes

Cat/Bear mouth

Rabbit mouth

Cat nose

Bear nose

Craft Activity: Examples

Ocean Water—Recipe

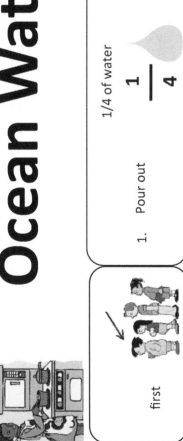

1. Pour out 1/4 of water $\frac{1}{4}$ from bottle

first

2. Add sugar (3 tbs)

3. Add blue food coloring (1 drop)

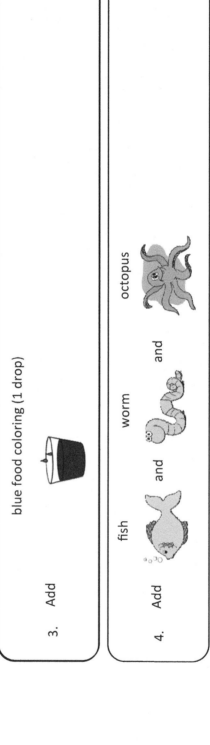

4. Add fish and worm and octopus

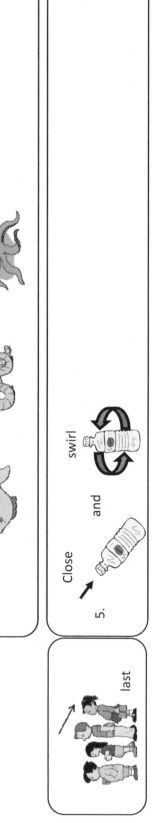

5. Close and swirl

last

Agua de océano—Receta

1. Quitar
   1/4 de agua $\frac{1}{}$ de
   botella

primero

2. Añadir
   3 cucharas de azúcar

3. Añadir
   colorante alimentico azul (1 drop)

4. Añadir
   pez   Y   gusano   Y   pulpo

5. Cerrar   Y   girar

al final

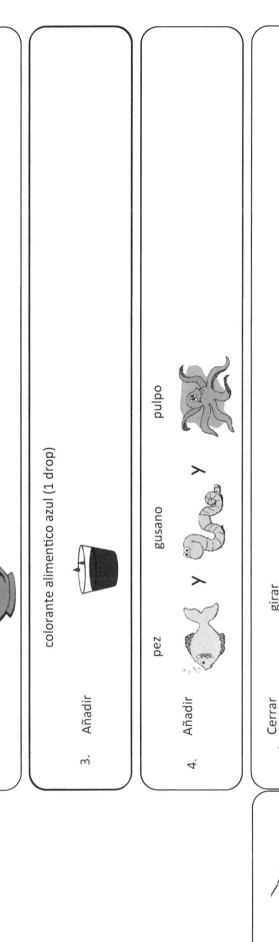

Unit 5

City and Country

La ciudad y el campo

CITY AND COUNTRY

Language Focus:

Identify objects/pictures given descriptive attributes.

Identify or use verbs in sentences.

Compare/contrast people, places, and things.

Answer who, what, where questions.

Curriculum Skills by Grade:

K.   Identify how the human characteristics of place, such as ways of earning a living, shelter, clothing, food and activities, are based on geographic location.

1.   Identify and describe how the human characteristics of place such as shelter, clothing, food and activities are based upon geographic location.

2.   Identify the characteristics of different communities, including urban, suburban, and rural, and how they affect activities.

3.   Identify and compare how people in different communities adapt to or modify the physical environment in which they live.

4.   Identify, locate, and compare geographic regions, including landforms, climate, and

5.   Describe a variety of regions in the U.S. that result from physical characteristics.

Suggested Songs:

English	Spanish
Color Farm	*Colores en la granja*
Wheels on the Bus	*Las ruedas del camión*

Materials	Recipe Ingredients (*per student)
Switch visuals for:	Graham cracker
City name	Chocolate frosting
Stop	M&Ms (green, red, yellow)
Go	Plastic knife
	Plate

Content

Section	Schedule	Activity	Goals
		Lesson 1 and 2	
5A	Surprise Bag	City and country things we see	• Identify pictures • Label • Formulate sentences • Expand utterances
5B	Song	Color Farm/Colores en la granja	• Answer questions • Label • Identify colors • Identify animals
5C	Sentence Strip	I like to _____ in _____. Me gusta _____ en _____.	• Express semantic relationships • Expand utterances
5D	Question of the Day	Cut out animal picture cards 1. Where do you live?/¿Dónde vives? 2. What do you do in the country?/¿Qué haces en el campo?	• Follow directions • Answer questions • Expand utterances
5E	Story	1. Life in the City/Mi vida en la ciudad A. Story board B. Story questions 2. My trip to the country/Mi viaje al campo A. Story board B. Story questions	• Identify places • Label places • Label actions • Increase vocabulary • Understand semantic relationships • Expand utterances

Content

5
CITY AND COUNTRY

Section	Schedule	Activity	Goals
		Lesson 1 and 2	
5F	Story Questions	Low-tech picture boards Story question pages Icon sentence strips	• Answer questions • Expand utterances
5G	Story Articulation	Story vocabulary listed by sound	• Practice articulation/ phonology
5H	Game	City and country bingo	• Follow directions • Identify people and places • Request • Understand semantic relationships
5I	Crafts	My home/Mi hogar	• Answer questions • Categorize • Label • Expand utterances
5J	Recipe	Stoplight	• Follow directions • Label items • Sequence • Expand utterances

Lesson Plan 1 (pg. 1 of 2)

Date:_____

Below is an example of a 90-minute speech therapy lesson plan. Modify this lesson plan as needed to fit your individual needs, including time in the classroom, student services recommended in the educational plan, and student goals.

5

CITY AND COUNTRY

Time	Schedule	Activity	Goals
15 min.	Discrete Trials	Preference assessment- refer to: Joint attention protocol Objects/visuals: locations, types of transportation May use objects that move to target 'stop' and 'go'	Increase joint attention skills Identify objects Take turns Practice articulation
15 min.	Question of the Day (QoD)	QoD: Where do you live? Clinician says "Today we are going to talk about places such as cities and the countryside. Goes around the room and asks "Where do you live?" Provide a visual of city and country. Ask a friend, "Where do you live?"	Identify phonemes Mark syllables Answer questions Increase joint attention Produce SVO sentences
5 min.	Language Goal	Clinician: ***Today we are going to learn about the city and the country.*** Clinician: ***What vehicles do we see in the country? In the city? What buildings do you see in the city?*** Assess prior knowledge.	1. Label: transportation, locations 2. Use prepositions: location 3. Produce/answer target questions:
15 min.	Surprise Bag	Place cards in the surprise bag. Clinician: ***Today we are talking about the city and the country. What do you think is in the bag?*** Pass the bag around and use the same sequence instruction for each student. ***Close your eyes. Put your hand in the bag. Take out your surprise.*** Clinician: ***What do you have?*** Student: _____ Clinician: ***Yes it is a _____. (follow up question)***	Name/label: animals and locations Follow directions

Date:_____

5 CITY AND COUNTRY

Time	Schedule	Activity	Goals
5 min.	Song	Introduce "Color Farm" song and vocabulary in the song. Have the students dance with the song, pairing gestures and pictures with key concepts.	Expand utterances: "I want + to sing + color farm"
15 min.	Story	Read the book *Life in the City* Use scaffolding techniques and the story board while reading the book.	Label locations Answer questions Produce SVO sentence structures
15 min.	Comprehension Questions	Students complete the worksheets to "test" what they have learned from the story. Provide worksheets with multiple choice modifications for students who need scaffolding support.	Answer questions Produce phrases/ sentences Use correct syntax (i.e., word order, obligatory words)
5 min.	Wrap Up and Clean Up	Review the language target and/or sound target. ***Today we learned about places, where they are, and what is near them.***	

Lesson Plan 2 (pg. 1 of 2)

Date:_____

Below is an example of a 90-minute speech therapy lesson plan. Modify this lesson plan as needed to fit your individual needs, including time in the classroom, student services recommended in the educational plan, and student goals.

5

CITY AND COUNTRY

Time	Schedule	Activity	Goals
15 min.	Discrete Trials	Preference assessment- refer to: Joint attention protocol Objects/visuals: animals, types of transportation	Increase joint attention skills Identify objects Take turns Practice articulation
15 min.	Question of the Day (QoD)	QoD: What do you do in the country? Clinician says: "Today we are going to talk about the country. She goes around the room and asks, 'What do you do in the country?'" Provide a visual of riding a horse, collecting eggs, and blank card for additional answers. Ask a friend, "What do you do in the country?"	Identify phonemes Mark syllables Answer questions Increase joint attention Produce SVO sentences
5 min.	Language Goal	Clinician: *Today, we are going to learn about the country.* Clinician: *What animals do we see in the country? What vehicles do we see in the country?* Assess prior knowledge.	1. Label: transportation, animals 2. Use verbs: animal actions 3. Answer target questions: _____
15 min.	Surprise Bag	Place cards in the surprise bag. Clinician: *Today we are talking about the country. What do you think is in the bag?* Pass the bag around and use the same sequence instruction for each student. *Close your eyes. Put your hand in the bag. Take out your surprise.* Clinician: *What do you have?* Student: _____ Clinician: *Yes it is a _____. (follow up question)*	Name animals and types of transportation Follow directions

Date:_____

5

CITY AND COUNTRY

Time	Schedule	Activity	Goals
10 min.	Song	Introduce "Color Farm" song and vocabulary in the song. Have the students dance with the song, pairing gestures and pictures with key concepts.	Expand utterances: "I want + to sing + color farm." "It is a (color)+(animal)."
15 min.	Story	Read the book *My Trip to the Country* Use scaffolding techniques and the story board while reading the book.	Label animals Answer questions Produce SVO sentence structures
15 min.	Comprehension Questions	Students complete the worksheets to "test" what they have learned from the story. Provide worksheets with multiple choice modifications for students who need scaffolding support.	Answer questions Produce phrases/sentences Use correct syntax (i.e., word order, obligatory words)
5 min.	Wrap Up and Clean Up	Review the language target and/or sound target. ***Today we learned about the country, what animals live there, and what types of transportation we see.***	

Modifications

Physical Impairments	Felt board to reduce travel and increase participation with large group., removable visuals using Velcro, flashlight for pointing.
AAC Devices	Visuals and Templates needed: 1. community-based locations/school locations 2. community members/family/ peers Switches- *Stop!, Go!, Where do you live?, Where should we go next?*
Visual Impairment	Objects: *Toy vehicles, farm animal toys*
Hearing Impairment	Signs: *city, country, car, horse, boy, girl* Visuals: see story boards and sentence strips
Behavior	Personal object/activity: Play Red Light, Green Light

Communication Abilities

Nonverbal	Joint attention Use picture/word/sign to request preferred object/activity Identify: *types of transportation, signs, traffic lights*
Nonverbal + Gestures	Follow directions: "stop," "go," "go to (location)" Imitate- CV, VCV, CVCV combinations English: *my, go, out, take, car, autobús, life, look, light, cow, house* Spanish: *mi, tu, el, la, alto, carro, bos, luz, mira, vida, vaca, casa*
Low Verbal- 1 Word	Produce- CV, VCV, CVCV combinations Label objects: *apartment, house, city, country, park, field, car, tractor, horse, cow, people, light* Target words: *stop, go*
Verbal	Expressive Goals: Increase MLU: prepositional phrases Sentence strip: "I like to (verb phrase) in the (location)."

Surprise Bag

apartment	city	country
apartamentos	*ciudad*	*campo*
house	park	cornfield
casa	*parque*	*campo de maíz*
car	tractor	horse
carro	*tractor*	*caballo*
people	stoplight	cow
gente	*semáforo*	*vaca*

Surprise Bag Sentence Strip

Use this sentence strip with the vocabulary on the preceding page.

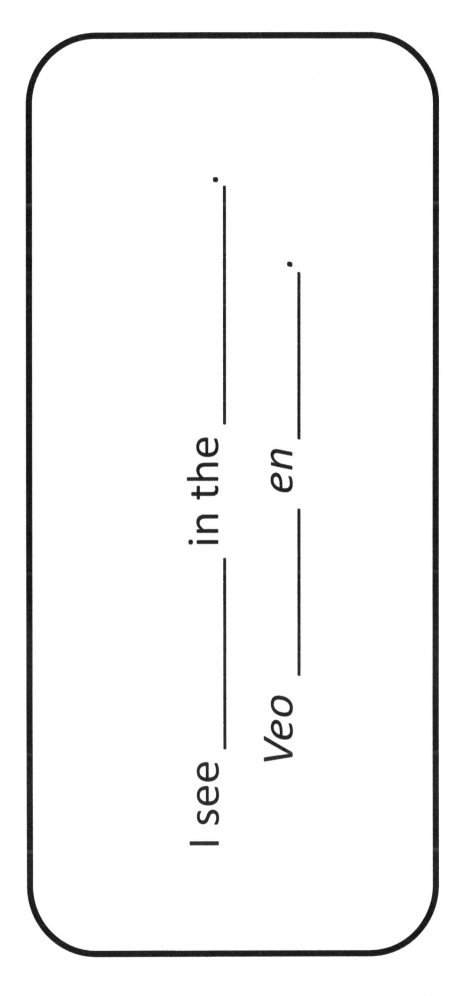

I see _____ in the _____.

Veo _____ en _____.

city

country

ride horses

milk cows

collect eggs

play hide and seek

pick corn

watch the stars

ride the bus

visit the library

put money in the bank

play in the park

go for a walk in the city

take a taxi

ride the tractor

5

English Sentence Strip

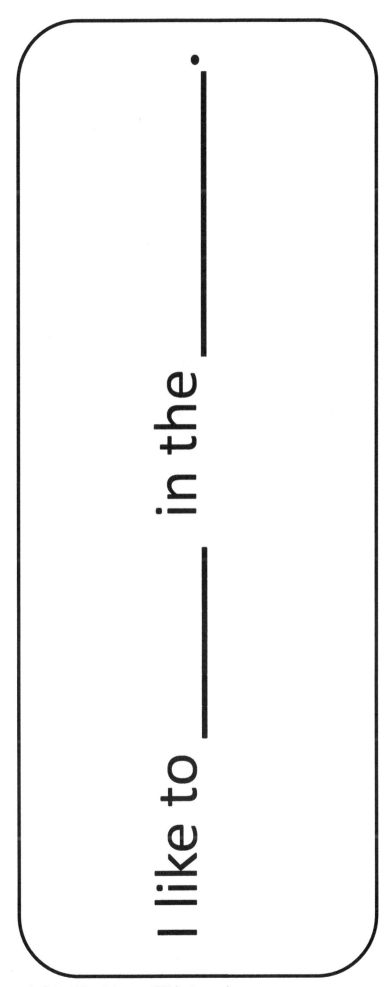

I like to _____ in the ___.

ciudad	campo	montar caballos
ordeñar vacas	recolectar huevos	jugar a las escondidas
cosechar maíz	mirar las estrellas	subir al autobús
visitar la bibliotéca	depositar dinero en el banco	jugar en el parque
caminar en la ciudad	tomar un taxi	manejar el tractor

5 CITY AND COUNTRY

 **Spanish Sentence Strip**

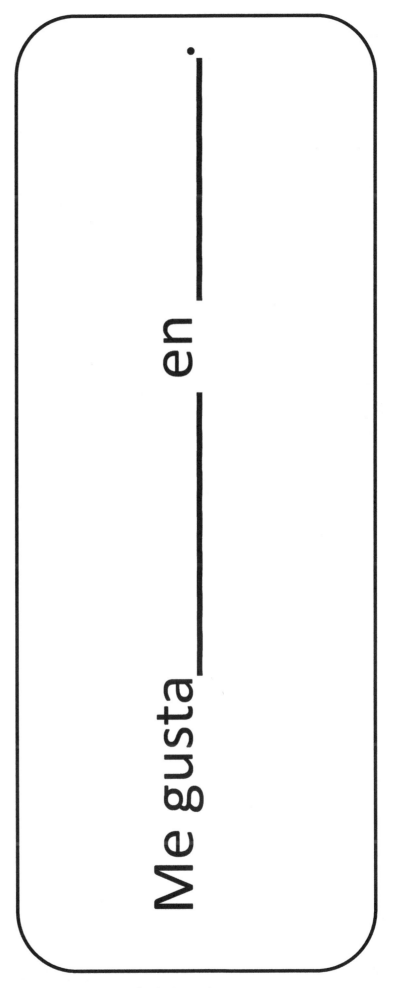

Me gusta _____ en _____.

Song

5

CITY AND COUNTRY

Song Activity: *Color Farm*

Colores en la Granja

Suggested goals to target:

- Label animals and colors
- Match colors
- Use descriptor + noun

Purpose:

- Use attached visual cues.
- Teach concepts prior to the song, reinforce concepts during the song, and review concepts after the song.
- Identify and label targeted vocabulary when learning the song's lyrics.
- Ask and answer questions, such as "What animal is black?"
- Sequence animals in the song (e.g. Which animal was first, next...?).
- Encourage and facilitate participation in group activities.
- Increase and maintain attention to group activities.

Suggested activities:

- Review the animals and the colors with the entire class.
- Compare colors with students' clothing. (e.g. "Who is wearing a purple shirt?").
- Ask questions (e.g. "Have you ever seen a purple cow?").
- Cut and place Velcro on pictures of animals with cards that are the same color as the animal so that students can work on matching and describing skills.

Song

cat	dog
gato	*perro*
horse	cow
caballo	*vaca*
bird	duck
pájaro	*pato*
chick	pig
pollito	*cerdo*

Question of the Day 1

where

do

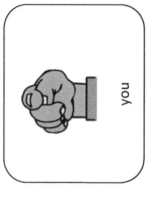

you

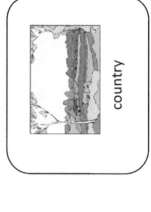

live

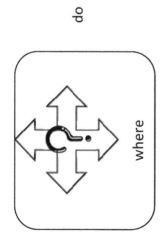

city

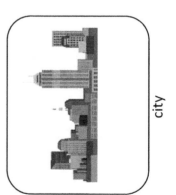

country

?.

5 CITY AND COUNTRY

La pregunta del día 1

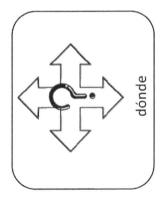

vivir

dónde

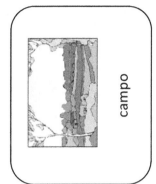

campo

ciudad

Story 1 / Cuento 1

Life in the City

Mi vida en la ciudad

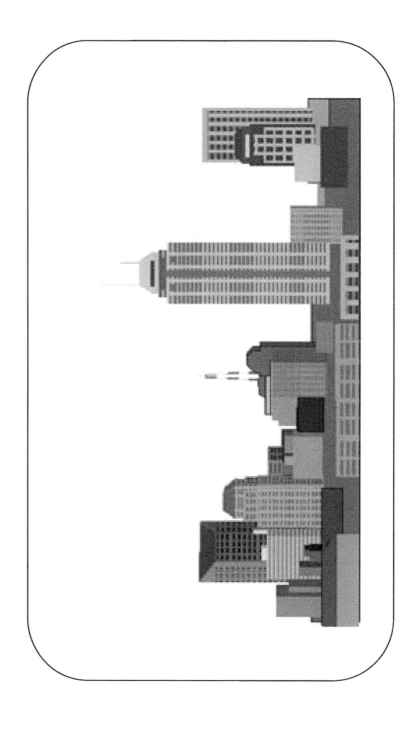

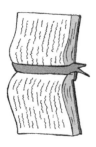

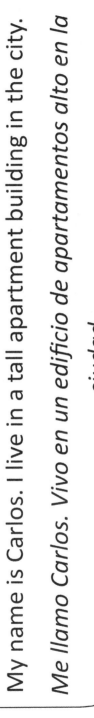

My name is Carlos. I live in a tall apartment building in the city.

Me llamo Carlos. Vivo en un edificio de apartamentos alto en la ciudad.

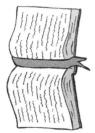

When I look out of my window, I see tall buildings, a lot of people, cars and buses.

Cuando miro por la ventana, yo veo edificios altos, mucha gente, carros, y autobuses.

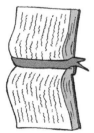

When I go outside, there are many people walking fast on the sidewalk.

Cuando salgo afuera, hay mucha gente caminando rápido por la banqueta.

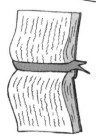

127

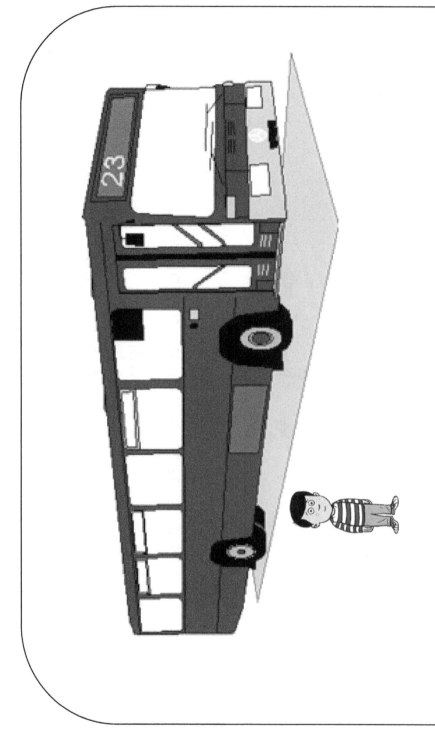

I take the bus to go places in the city.

Me subo al autobús para ir a diferentes lugares en la ciudad.

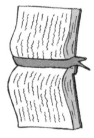

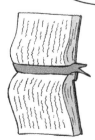

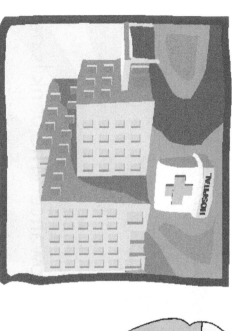

I visit the library to check out a book. The library is next to the hospital.

Visito la biblioteca para sacar un libro. La biblioteca está al lado del hospital.

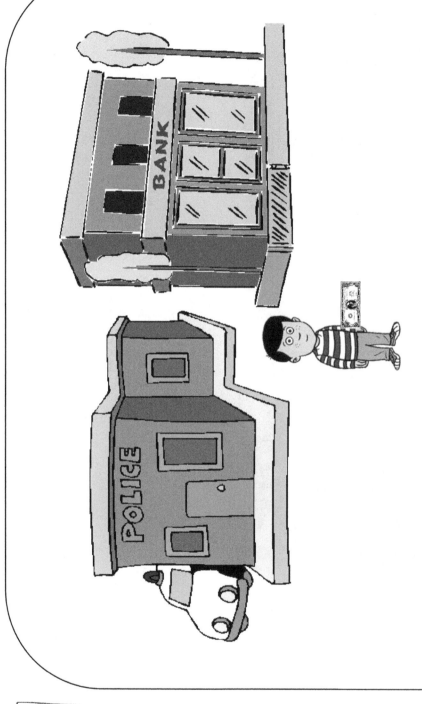

I visit the bank to deposit my allowance. The bank is next to the police station.

Visito el banco para depositar mi dinero. El banco está al lado de la estación de policía.

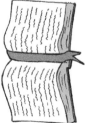

I visit the park to play with my friends. The park is next to my school.

Visito el parque para jugar con mis amigos. El parque está al lado de mi escuela.

It is late. It is time to go back to my apartment.

Es tarde. Es hora de regresar a mi apartamento.

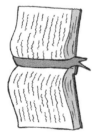

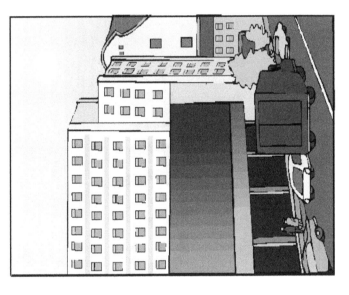

The city is filled with many people and tall buildings. I like living in the city.

La ciudad está llena de mucha gente y edificios altos. Me gusta vivir en la ciudad.

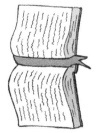

The End

El fin

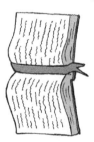

Life in the City

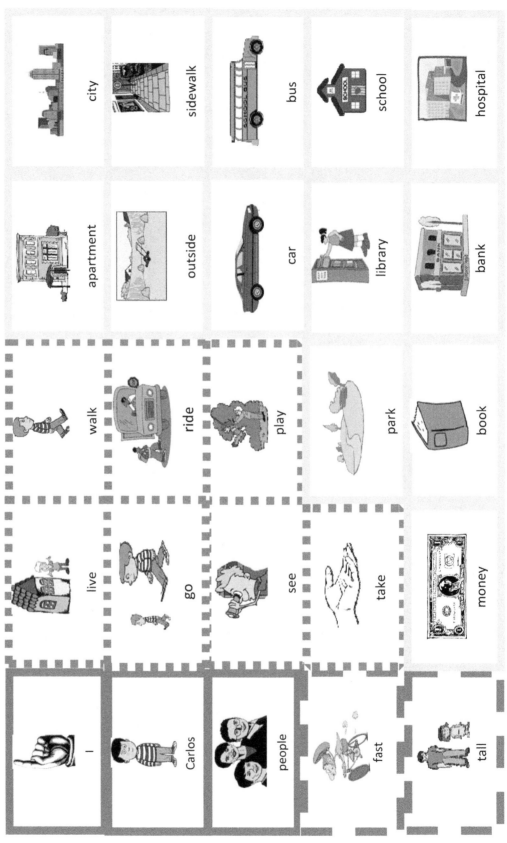

Mi vida en la ciudad

No

Sí

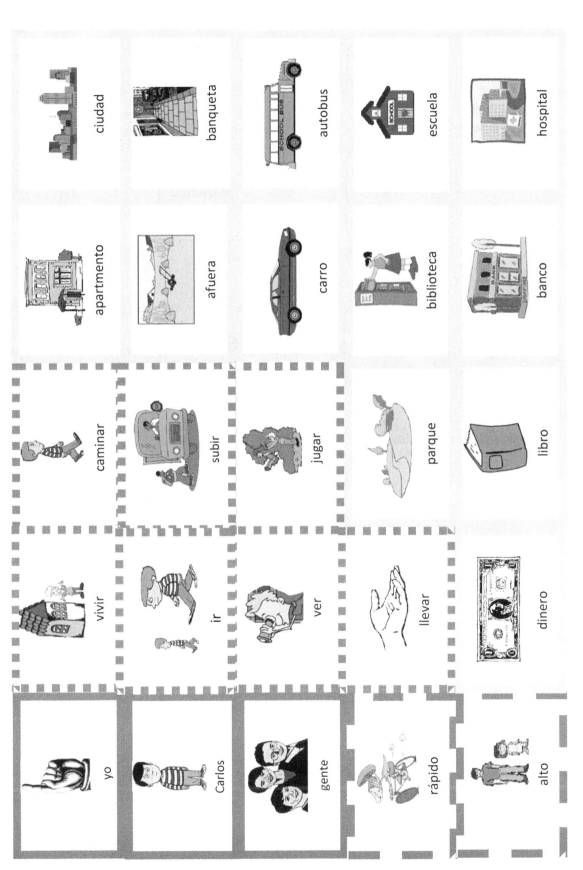

ciudad

banqueta

autobus

escuela

hospital

apartmento

afuera

carro

biblioteca

banco

caminar

subir

jugar

parque

libro

vivir

ir

ver

llevar

dinero

yo

Carlos

gente

rápido

alto

Story 1 Questions

Life in the City

1. Where does Carlos live?

farm

house

apartment

2. What does Carlos see when he looks outside?

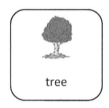

tree

car

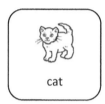

cat

3. Which place did Carlos visit?

bank

zoo

movie theater

4. Where did Carlos check out a book?

park

library

hospital

5. What did Carlos do with his friends in the park?

read

sleep

play

Story 1 Questions

Life in the City

5 CITY AND COUNTRY

1. Where does Carlos live?

2. What does Carlos see when he looks outside?

3. Which place did Carlos visit?

4. Where did Carlos check out a book?

5. What did Carlos do with his friends in the park?

Preguntas del cuento 1

Mi vida en la ciudad

1. ¿Dónde vive Carlos?

 granja    casa    apartmento

2. ¿Qué ve Carlos cuando mira afuera?

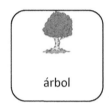 árbol    carro    gato

3. ¿A cuál lugar visita Carlos?

 banco   zoológico    cine

4. ¿Dónde sacó el libro?

 parque    biblioteca    hospital

5. ¿Qué hizo Carlos en el parque con sus amigos?

 leer    dormir    jugar

Preguntas del cuento 1

Mi vida en la ciudad

1. ¿Dónde vive Carlos?

2. ¿Qué ve Carlos cuando mira afuera?

3. ¿A cuál lugar visita Carlos?

4. ¿Dónde sacó el libro?

5. ¿Qué hizo Carlos en el parque con sus amigos?

English Articulation Words

5 CITY AND COUNTRY

Story 1: Life in the City

English

M my, many, name, apartment, time

N name, next, many, when, station, apartment, window

P park, people, police, apartment, hospital, deposit, play, people, places

K car, Carlos, book, look, back, bank, walk, take, like, check, sidewalk, park, school

G go, building, walking

T tall, take, time, city, outside, apartment, hospital, out, lot, late, visit, deposit, out, fast, next, apartment

D deposit, sidewalk, filled, building, window

F fast, filled, life, friends

S city, see, sidewalk, outside, places, visit, hospital, deposit, friends, buildings, bus, places, police, Carlos, fast, school, station

L life, live, late, look, like, library, filled, police, allowance, tall, school, hospital, play, building, people

R library, car, friends, apartment, park

Sonidos del habla—Español

Cuento 1 Mi vida en la ciudad

5

CITY AND COUNTRY

Spanish

M miro, apartamentos, caminando, amigos

N lleno, ventana, dinero, caminando, con, estación, cuando, ventana

P por, para, parque, policía, rápido, depositar, apartamentos, hospital

B banco, banqueta, biblioteca, subió, autobuses, libro, biblioteca

K con, cuando, carros, carlos, caminando, sacar, biblioteca, escuela

G amigos, gusta, regresar, lugar

T tarde, visitó, banqueta, hospital, autobuses, biblioteca, depositar, está, gusta, altos, estación, apartamentos

D de, dinero, diferentes, depositar, vida, lado, ciudad, rápido, edificio, ciudad, cuando

F diferentes, afuera

S subo, ciudad, sacar, visitó, regresar, autobuses, depositar, estación, policía, altos, carros, carlos, amigos, autobuses, diferentes, está, gusta, hospital, escuela, estación

L lugar, libro, lado, policía, hospital, escuela, altos, biblioteca

R rápido, regresar, miro, afuera, para, hora, diferentes, por, depositar, lugar, sacar, jugar, vivir, ir, libro, apartamentos

Question of the Day 2

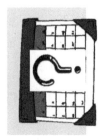

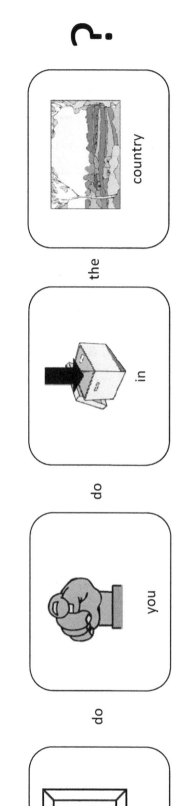

What | do | you | do | in | the | country | ?

ride a horse

collect eggs

?.

La pregunta del día 2

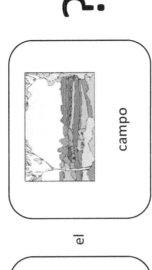

el

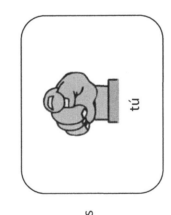

campo

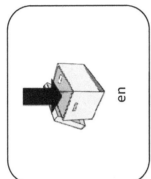

en

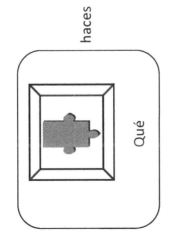

tú

haces

Qué

montar caballo

colectar huevos

Story 2 / Cuento 2

My Trip to the Country.

Mi viaje al campo.

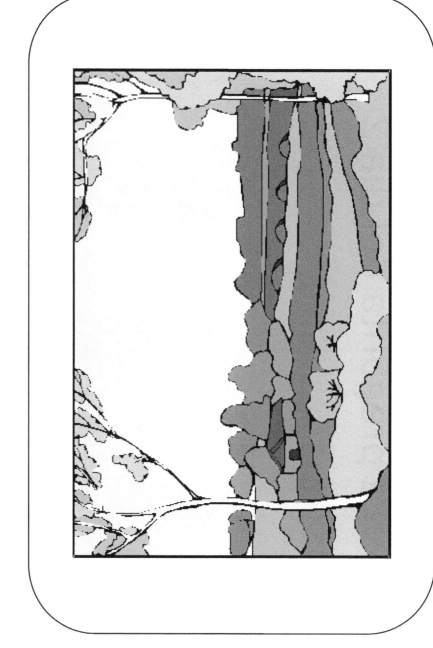

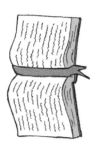

I live in the city. My friend, Maria, lives in the country.

I like to visit Maria at her house in the country.

Yo vivo en la ciudad. Mi amiga, María, vive en el campo. Me gusta visitar a María en su casa en el campo.

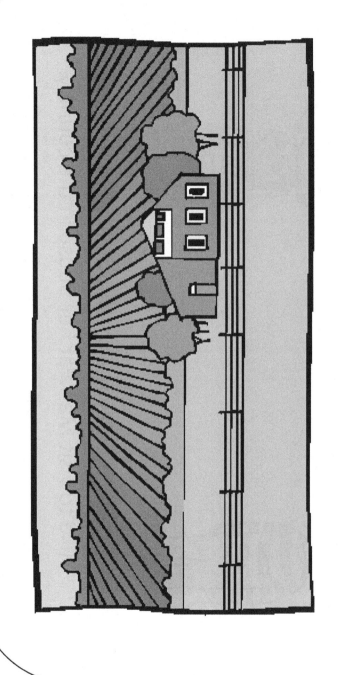

Out in the country, what do we see? We see open fields and lots of trees. Maria and I run and play in the field.

Allá en el campo, ¿qué es lo que vemos? El campo abierto y muchos árboles. María y yo corremos y jugamos en el campo.

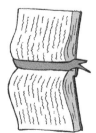

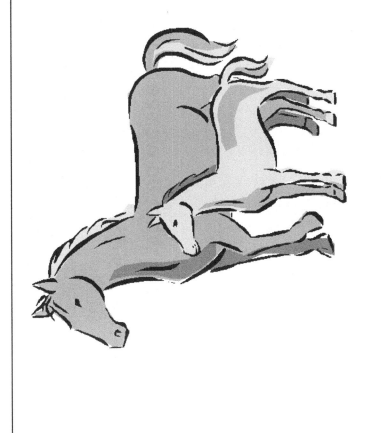

Out in the country, what do we see? We see horses. Maria and I ride the horses.

Allá en el campo, ¿qué es lo que vemos? Vemos caballos. María y yo montamos los caballos.

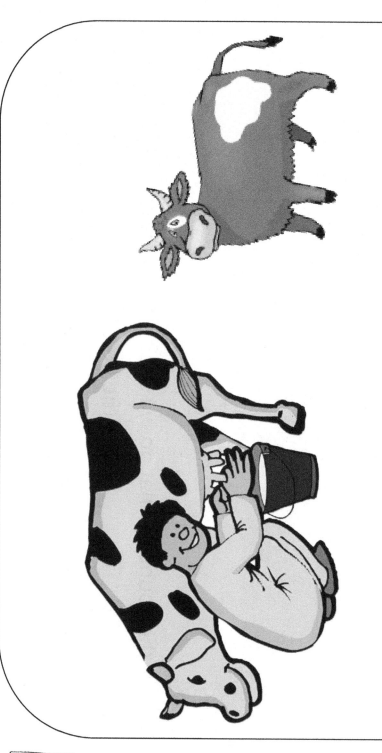

Out in the country, what do we see? We see cows.

Maria's dad milks the cows.

Allá en el campo, ¿qué es lo que vemos? Vemos vacas.

El papá de María ordeña las vacas.

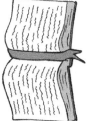

Out in the country, what do we see? We see chickens.

Maria and I help collect eggs.

Allá en el campo, ¿qué es lo que vemos? Vemos gallinas. María

y yo ayudamos a colectar los huevos.

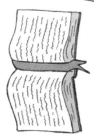

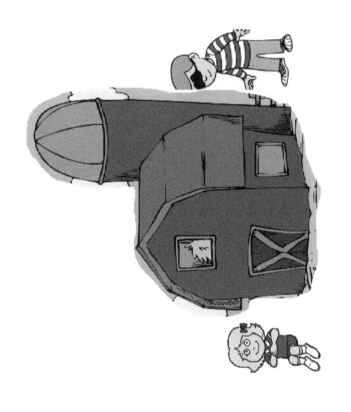

Out in the country, what do we see? We see an old barn.

Maria and I play hide and seek in the barn.

Allá en el campo, ¿qué es lo que vemos? Vemos un granero viejo. María y yo jugamos a las escondidas en el granero.

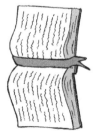

Out in the country, what do we see? We see a big tractor.
Maria's dad drives the tractor.

Allá en el campo, ¿qué es lo que vemos? Vemos un tractor gran-
de. El papá de María maneja el tractor.

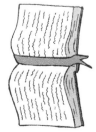

153

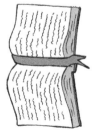

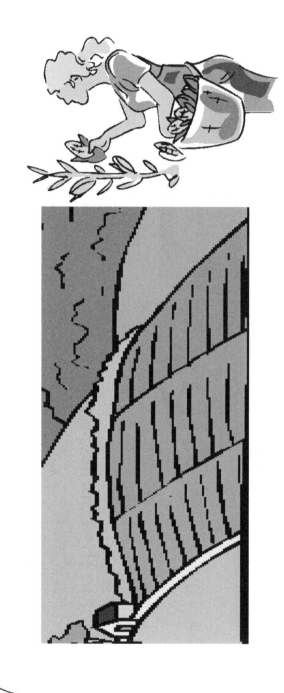

Out in the country, what do we see? We see a cornfield. Maria's mom picks corn for dinner.

Allá en el campo, ¿qué es lo que vemos? Vemos un campo de maíz. La mamá de María cosecha maíz para la cena.

Out in the country, what do we see? We see many bright stars at night. It is time for bed.

Allá en el campo, ¿qué es lo que vemos? Vemos muchas estrellas brillantes en la noche. Es hora de dormir.

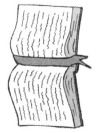

The End

El fin

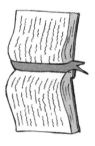

My Trip to the Country

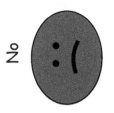

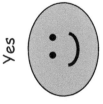

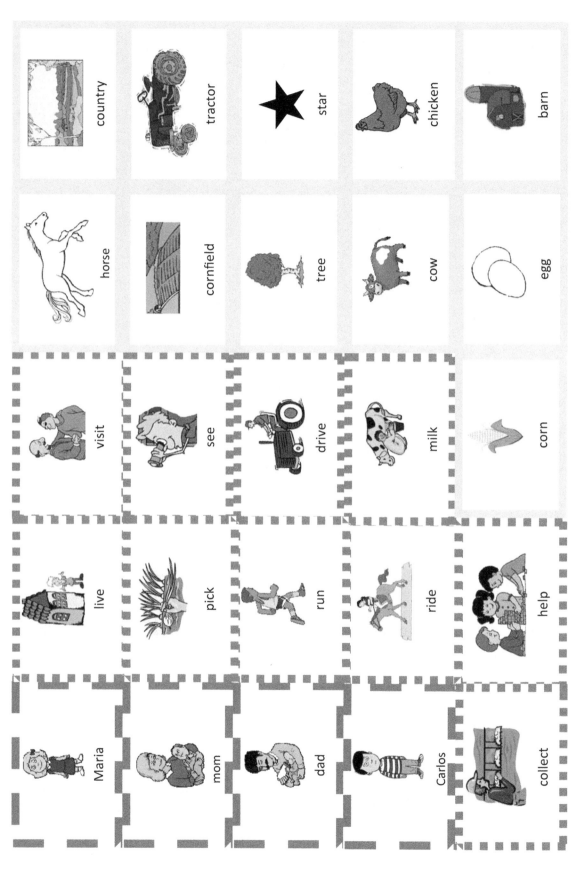

country	horse	Maria	live
tractor	cornfield	mom	pick
star	tree	dad	run
chicken	cow	Carlos	ride
barn	egg	collect	help
	corn		

visit
see
drive
milk
corn

Mi viaje al campo

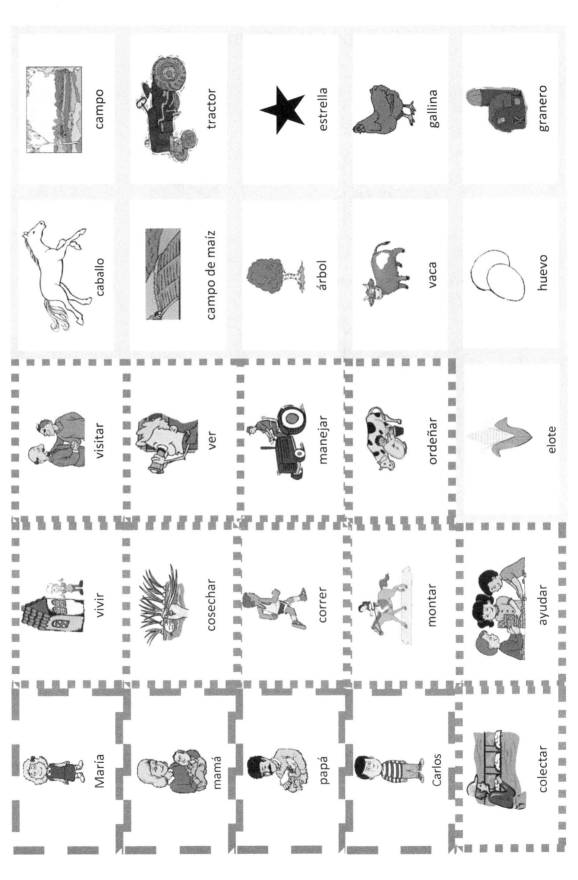

campo

tractor

estrella

gallina

granero

caballo

campo de maíz

árbol

vaca

huevo

visitar

ver

manejar

ordeñar

elote

vivir

cosechar

correr

montar

ayudar

María

mamá

papá

Carlos

colectar

Story 2 Questions

My Trip to the Country

1. Where does Maria live?

 country    school    city

2. What do you see in the country?

 soda    taxi   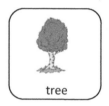 tree

3. What do the chickens lay?

 turnip    egg    block

4. Who drives the tractor?

 Maria    mom    dad

5. When do we see stars?

 day    night    rain

Story 2 Questions

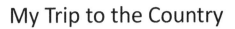

My Trip to the Country

5 **CITY AND COUNTRY**

1. Where does Maria live?

2. What do we see in the country?

3. What do chickens lay?

4. Who drives the tractor?

5. When do we see stars?

Preguntas del cuento 2

Mi viaje el campo

1. ¿Dónde vive María?

campo

escuela

ciudad

2. ¿Qué vemos en el campo?

soda

taxi

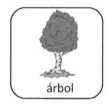
árbol

3. ¿Qué ponen las gallinas?

nabo

huevo

bloque

4. ¿Quién maneja el tractor?

Maria

mama

papa

5. ¿Cuándo vemos las estrellas?

dia

noche

lluvia

Preguntas del cuento 2

Mi viaje el campo

5

CITY AND COUNTRY

1. ¿Dónde vive María?

2. ¿Qué vemos en el campo?

3. ¿Qué ponen las gallinas?

4. ¿Quién maneja el tractor?

5. ¿Cuándo vemos las estrellas?

English Articulation Words **5**

Story 2: My Trip to the Country.

English

M milks, many, Maria, mom, time

N night, dinner, open, barn, corn, chicken

P pick, open, trip, help, play

K cows, corn, collect, country, cornfield, chicken, like, seek, pick

G eggs, big

T time, city, out, what, bright, night, visit, trip, trees, stars, country, tractor

D do, dad, dinner, ride, old, hide, bed, friend, fields

F fields, for, cornfield, friend

S see, city, seek, visit, horses, house, lots, milks, horses, stars

L run, ride, Maria, horses, her, for, tractor, dinner, trip, trees, bright, country, friend

R live, like, lots, collect, fields, play

Spanish

M campo, **m**ontar, **m**anejar, dor**m**ir, **m**aíz, **M**aría

P **p**apá, **p**ara, cam**p**o

B a**b**ierto, **b**rillantes, ár**b**oles, ca**b**allos, **b**rillantes

K **qu**e, **c**ampo, **c**asa, **c**orrer, **c**aballos, **c**olectar, **c**osechar, va**c**as, tra**c**tor, es**c**ondidas

G **g**rande, **g**allinas, **g**ranero, **g**usta, ju**g**ar

N **n**oche, esco**n**didas, mo**n**tar, gra**n**de, galli**n**as, ma**n**ejar, gra**n**ero, brilla**n**tes, ce**n**a, e**n**

T brillan**t**es, visi**t**or, abier**t**o, mon**t**ar, colec**t**ar, gus**t**a, **t**ractor, estrellas

D **d**e, **d**ormir, gran**d**e, or**d**eñar, ayu**d**ar, escon**did**as, ciu**dad**

S **s**u, **c**ena, **c**iudad, gu**s**ta, ca**s**a, vi**s**itor, co**s**echar, e**s**trella**s**, e**s**condida**s**, e**s**, maí**z**, vaca**s**, mucho**s**, huevo**s**, árbole**s**, caballo**s**, gallina**s**

L **l**a, **l**os, **l**as, árbo**l**es, co**l**ectar, e**l**

R ho**r**a, co**rr**er, do**r**mir, Ma**r**ía, abie**r**to, á**r**boles, o**r**deñar, g**r**ane**r**o, ve**r**, monta**r**, juga**r**, t**r**acto**r**, cosecha**r**, ayuda**r**, maneja**r**, colecta**r**, visito**r**, g**r**ande, est**r**ellas, b**r**illantes

Game: City and Country Bingo

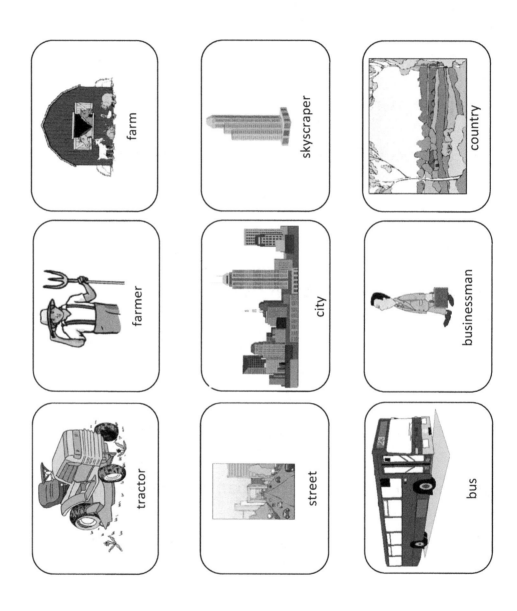

farm	farmer	tractor
skyscraper	city	street
country	businessman	bus

Game: City and Country Bingo

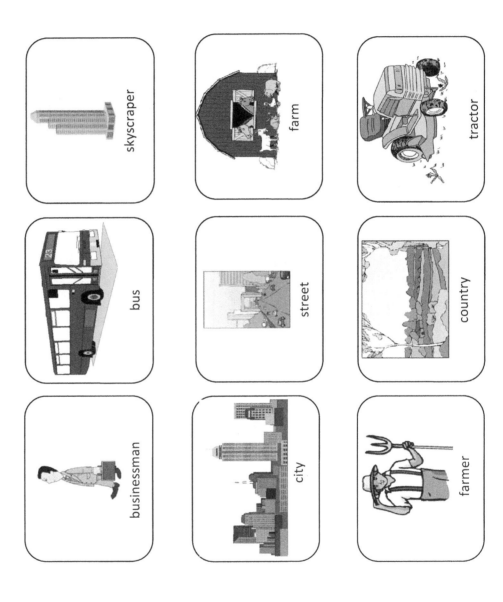

skyscraper

farm

tractor

bus

street

country

businessman

city

farmer

Game: City and Country Bingo

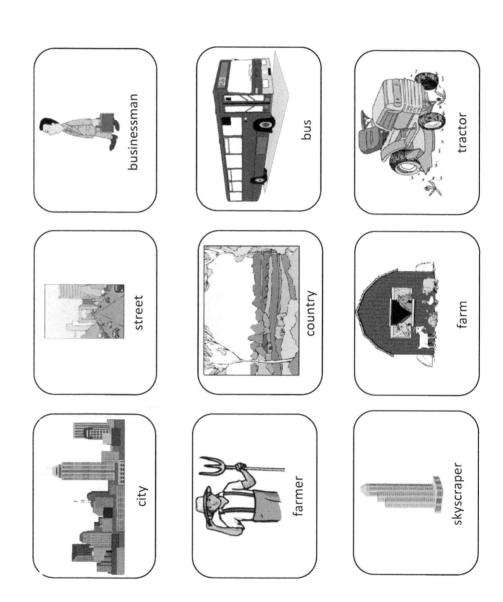

Game: City and Country Bingo

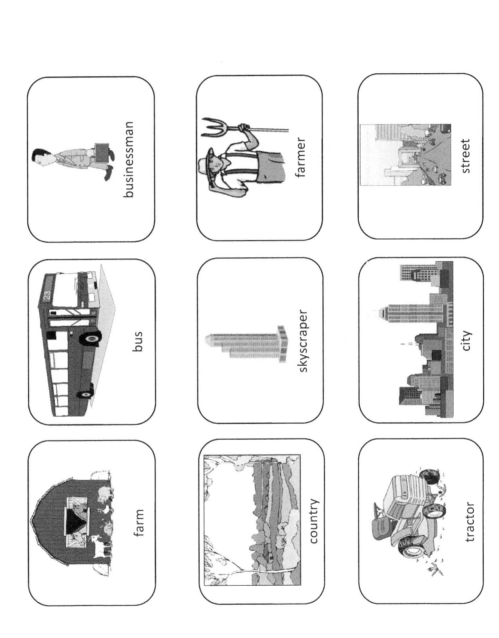

businessman	bus	farm
farmer	skyscraper	country
street	city	tractor

Juego: Bingo de ciudad y campo

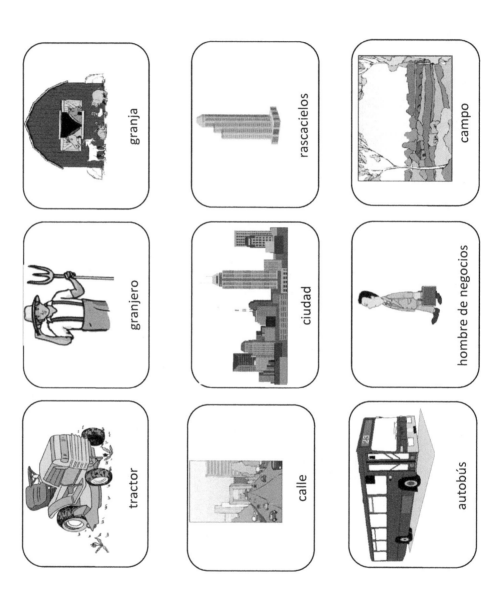

granja

granjero

tractor

rascacielos

ciudad

calle

campo

hombre de negocios

autobús

Juego: Bingo de ciudad y campo

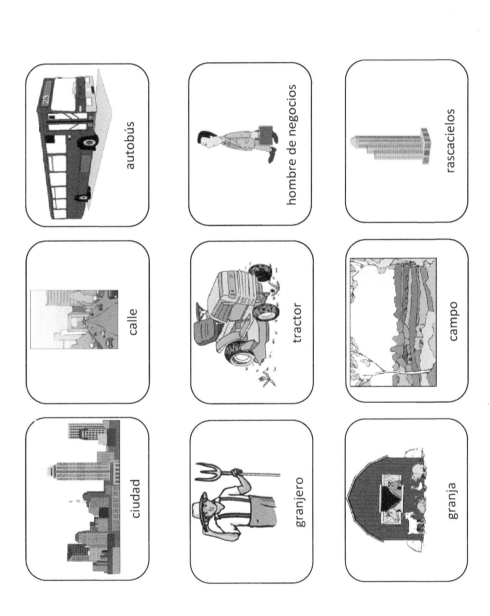

autobús

hombre de negocios

rascacielos

calle

tractor

campo

ciudad

granjero

granja

171

Juego: Bingo de ciudad y campo

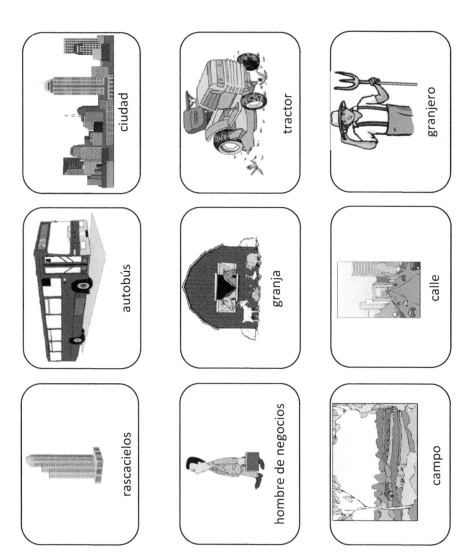

ciudad

tractor

granjero

autobús

granja

calle

rascacielos

hombre de negocios

campo

Juego: Bingo de ciudad y campo

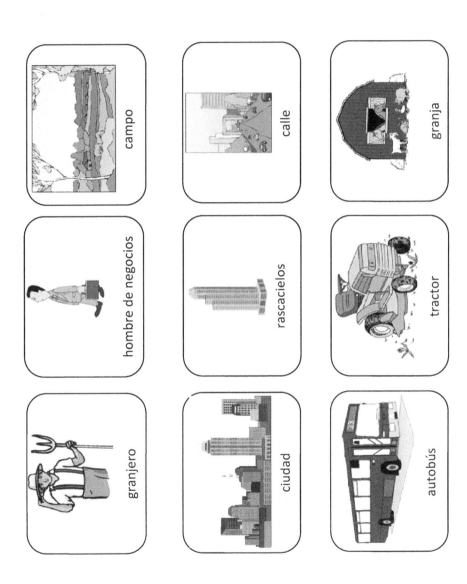

campo

calle

granja

hombre de negocios

rascacielos

tractor

granjero

ciudad

autobús

Craft Activity: My Home

first

1. Cut out   a   house   OR   apartment.

2. Glue   it on your   paper

3. Cut   tree   sun   clouds

4. Cut   bicycle   car   stop sign   fire hydrant

5. Glue   items   next to   house   OR   apartment

last

Arte: Mi Hogar

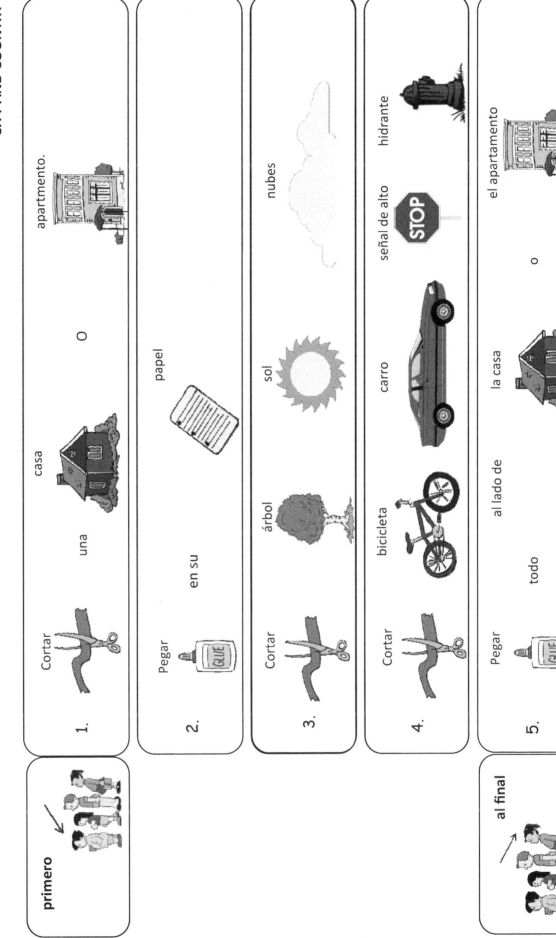

primero

1. Cortar una casa o apartmento.

2. Pegar en su papel

3. Cortar árbol sol nubes

4. Cortar bicicleta carro señal de alto hidrante

5. Pegar todo al lado de la casa o el apartamento

al final

Craft Activity: My Home

Stop sign

Sun

Fire hydrant

Tree

Bicycle

House   Apartment

Car

Clouds

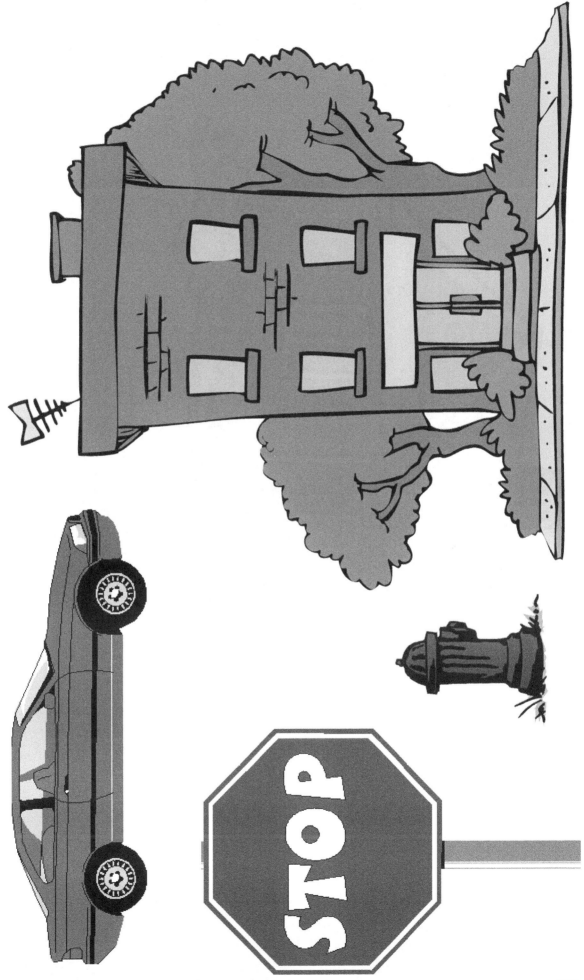

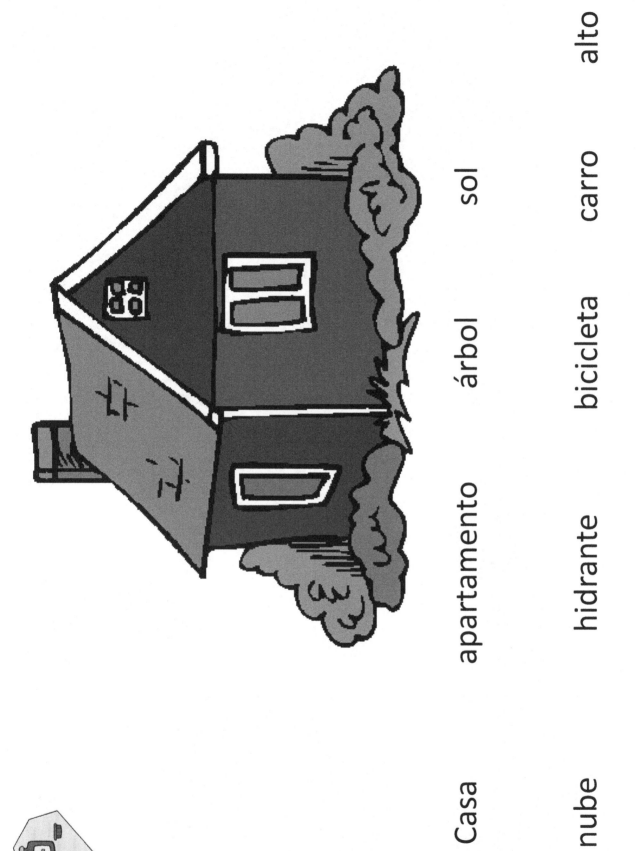

alto

sol   carro

árbol   bicicleta

apartamento   hidrante

Casa   nube

Recipe: Traffic Light

1. Take a graham cracker

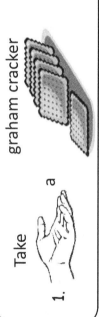

first

2. Put chocolate frosting on the graham cracker

3. Choose a green yellow and red M&Ms

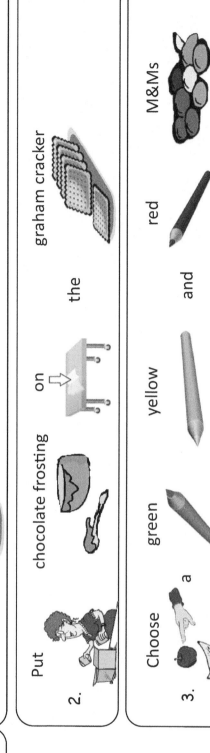

4. Put the graham cracker

5. Eat your traffic light

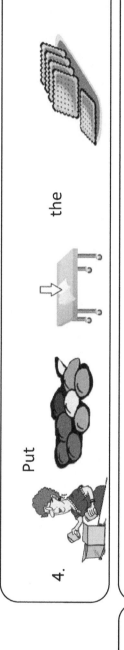

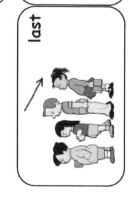

last

Receta: Semáforo

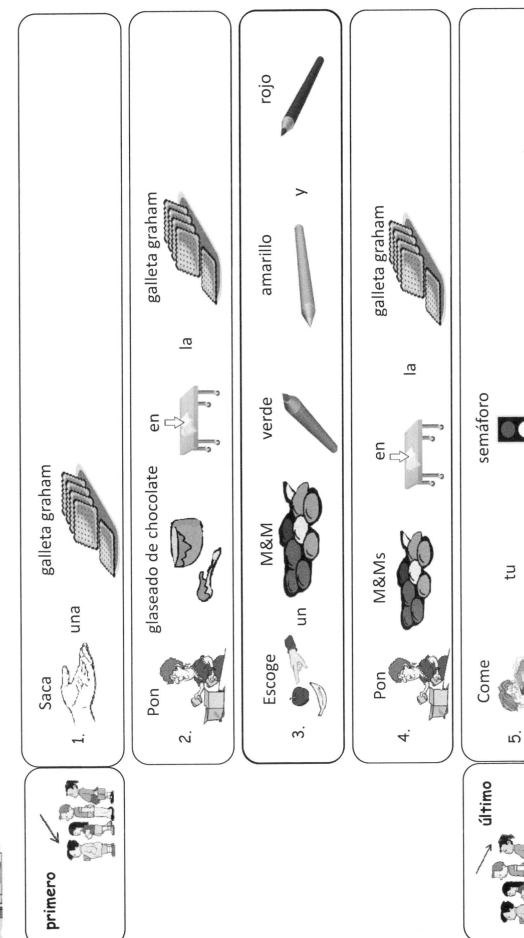

primero

1. Saca una galleta graham

2. Pon glaseado de chocolate en la galleta graham

3. Escoge un M&M verde amarillo y rojo

4. Pon M&Ms en la galleta graham

5. Come tu semáforo

último

Unit 6

Seasons and Sky

Las estaciones y el cielo

SEASONS AND SKY

Language Focus:

Label objects

Answer questions

Use descriptive words (ex: hot, cold, clear, cloudy, calm, windy)

Curriculum Skills by Grade:

K. Observe and describe weather changes from day to day and over seasons.

1. Record weather information, including relative temperature, such as hot or cold, clear or cloudy, calm or windy, and rainy or icy.

2. Identify the importance of weather and seasonal information to make choices in clothing, activities, and transportation.

3. Observe, measure, record, and compare day-to-day weather changes in different locations at the same time that include air temperature, wind direction, and precipitation.

4. Measure and record changes in weather and make predictions using weather maps, weather symbols, and a map key.

5. Differentiate between weather and climate.

Suggested Songs:

English	Spanish
Twinkle, Twinkle Little Star	Brilla, brilla estrellita
The Weather Song	La canción del tiempo
Months of the Year	Meses del año

Materials	Recipe Ingredients
	(*per student)
1. finger-paint (red, orange, yellow, green, blue, indigo, violet)	1 c milk
	2 tbs chocolate powder
2. cotton balls	5 marshmallows
3. glue	1 spoon
	1 cup

Content

6

SEASONS AND SKY

Section	Schedule	Activity **Lesson 1 and 2**	Goals
6A	Surprise Bag	Objects in the sky/seasons	• Increase vocabulary • Follow directions • Label • Expand utterances
6B	Song	Months of the year Meses del año	• Label • Sequence • Match • Categorize
6C	Sentence Strip	I see ____ in the sky. I like to ____ in the ____.	• Follow directions • Use adjectives • Expand utterances
6D	Question of the Day	1. Do you like daytime/nighttime? 2. What is your favorite season?	• Follow directions • Request • Ask questions • Categorize • Expand utterances
6E	Story	1. In the Sky 2. The Four Seasons	• Answer questions • Categorize • Label • Use adjectives • Expand utterances

Content

SEASONS AND SKY

Section	Schedule	Activity	Goals
		Lesson 1 and 2	
6F	Story Questions	1. In the Sky 2. The Four Seasons	• Answer questions • Create statements with negatives
6G	Story Articulation	English: /b, p, w, k, g, d, f, s, r. l, sh, ch/ Spanish: /p, b, m, n, k, f, x, ll, ñ, s, l, r/	• Practice Articulation • Use sentences from the story that include target sounds
6H	Game	Seasons and the Sky Bingo Switches: *Bingo!, Next, I'm so close!*	• Follow directions • Identify objects • Label
6I	Crafts	Fingerprint Rainbow Switches: *I need more paint!, This is messy!, Clean up on aisle 5.*	• Follow directions • Describe using colors • Request • Expand utterances
6J	Recipe	Hot Chocolate Switches: *Careful!, Is it too hot?!, This is delicious!*	• Follow directions • Qualitative concept (hot/cold) • Identify and name ingredients • Request • Use adjectives

Lesson Plan 1 (pg. 1 of 2)

Date:_____

Below is an example of a 90-minute speech therapy lesson plan. Modify this lesson plan as needed to fit your individual needs, including time in the classroom, student services recommended in the educational plan, and student goals.

6 SEASONS AND SKY

Time	Schedule	Activity	Goals
15 min.	Discrete Trials	Preference assessment- Joint attention protocol Objects/visuals: things we see in the sky (sun, stars)	Increase joint attention skills Identify objects Take turns Practice articulation
15 min.	Question of the Day (QoD)	QoD: Do you like daytime or nighttime? Clinician says, "Today we are going to talk about the sky. The sky changes during the day and at night." Clinician goes around the room and asks, "Do you like daytime or nighttime?" Provide a visual of a sun (daytime scene) and a moon (nighttime scene) Ask a friend, "What do you like best?" Optional follow-up: "Why?" Optional: Take a poll and compare how many students like daytime and how many like night time.	Identify phonemes Mark syllables Answer questions Increase joint attention Use phrases and sentences
5 min.	Language Goal	Clinician: *Today, we are going to learn about what we see in the sky.* Clinician: *What vehicles do we see in the sky? What animals do we see? And weather?* Assess prior knowledge.	1. Label: objects and weather related nouns 2. Use prepositions: location 3. Answer target questions: _____

Date:_____

6

SEASONS AND SKY

Time	Schedule	Activity	Goals
15 min.	Surprise Bag	Place cards in the surprise bag. Clinician: *Today we are talking about the sky. What do you think is in the bag?* Pass the bag around and use the same sequence instruction for each student. *Close your eyes. Put your hand in the bag. Take out your surprise.* Clinician: *What do you have?* Student: _____ Clinician: *Yes it is a _____. (follow up question)*	Name objects in the sky Follow directions
5 min.	Song	Introduce "Months of the year" song and vocabulary in the song. Have the students dance with the song, pairing gestures with key concepts	Expand utterances: "I want + to sing + months of the year." Answer questions
15 min.	Story	Read the book *In the sky* Use scaffolding techniques and the story board while reading the book.	Label things in the sky Answer questions Use SVO sentence structures
15 min.	Comprehension Questions	Students complete the worksheets to "test" what they have learned from the story. Provide worksheets with multiple choice modifications for students who need scaffolding support.	Answer questions Produce phrases/sentences Use correct syntax (i.e., word order, obligatory words)
5 min.	Wrap-Up and Clean Up	Review the language target and/or sound target. *Today we learned about what we see in the sky.*	

Lesson Plan 2 (pg. 1 of 2)

Date:_____

Below is an example of a 90-minute speech therapy lesson plan. Modify this lesson plan as needed to fit your individual needs, including time in the classroom, student services recommended in the educational plan, and student goals.

6

SEASONS AND SKY

Time	Schedule	Activity	Goals
15 min.	Discrete Trials	Preference assessment: Joint attention protocol Objects and visuals: weather simulation- *spray bottle, fan, warming pad*	Increase joint attention skills Identify objects Take turns Request
15 min.	Question of the Day (QoD)	QoD: What is your favorite season? Clinician says, "Today we are going to talk about the four seasons. The weather changes when the seasons change." Review the four seasons and weather associated with the seasons. Ask each student, "What is your favorite season?" Provide visual scenes or objects representing each season. Ask a friend, "What is your favorite season?" Optional follow-up: "Why?" Optional: Talk about holidays that occur during each season.	Identify phonemes Mark syllables Answer questions Increase joint attention Use phrase/sentence
5 min.	Language goal	Clinician: ***Today we are going to learn about the four seasons. What happens during winter? Summer?*** Assess prior knowledge.	1. Label: scenes and weather related nouns 2. Use adjectives 3. Answer target questions:

Lesson Plan 2 (pg. 2 of 2)

Date:_____

SEASONS AND SKY

Time	Schedule	Activity	Goals
15 min.	Surprise Bag	Place cards in surprise bag. Clinician: **Today, we are talking about the seasons. What do you think is in the bag?** Pass the bag around and use the same sequence instruction for each student. **Close your eyes. Put your hand in the bag. Take out your surprise.** Clinician: **What do you have?** Student: _____ Clinician: **Yes it is a _____. (follow up question)**	Name objects in the sky Follow directions
5 min.	Song	Introduce "Months of the year" song and vocabulary in the song. Have the students dance with the song, pairing gestures with key concepts.	Categorize months/seasons Expand utterances: "I want + to sing + months of the year"
15 min.	Story	Read the book *The Four Seasons* Use scaffolding techniques and the story board while reading the book.	Label the scenes Answer questions Expand utterances
15 min.	Comprehension Questions	Students complete the worksheets to "test" what they have learned from the story. Provide worksheets with multiple choice modifications for students who need scaffolding support.	Answer questions Produce phrases/sentences Use correct syntax (i.e., word order, obligatory words)
5 min.	Wrap-Up and Clean Up	Review the language target and/or sound target. **Today, we learned about the four seasons.**	

Modifications

Physical Impairments– Low Mobility	Modification: Felt/dry erase board in order to reduce travel, hand print or brush for craft activity
AAC Devices	Visuals and Templates needed: 1. weather template 2. calendar template Switches- *Bingo!, Next, I'm so close!, I need more paint!* *This is messy!, Clean up on aisle 5.* *Careful!, Is it too hot?!, This is delicious!*
Visual Impairment	Objects: *images of seasons, leaves, spray bottle, fan, faux flower, flashlight, bag of ice, heating pad*
Hearing Impairment	Signs: *hot/cold, light/dark* Visuals: *story boards and sentence strips*
Behavior	Personal object/activity: Calendar helper Weather reporter as a reward for positive behavior

Communication Abilities

Nonverbal	Joint attention Use picture/word/sign to request preferred object/activity Identify: *seasons, weather, objects in the sky, temperatures (hot/cold), qualitative concepts (light/dark)*
Nonverbal + Gestures	Follow directions: directions during surprise bag activity, "Go to the window", "Look out the window", etc. Imitate- CV, VCV, CVCV combinations English: *up, go, do, down, moon, sun, ship, light, night, white, rain, red, blue* Spanish: *que, veo, ver, por, mis, mas, sol, luz, hace, rojo, azul, sigue*
Low Verbal- 1 Word	Produce- CV, VCV, CVCV combinations Label objects: *sun, moon, star, cloud, rain, snow, wind, rain, winter, summer, spring, fall, rainbow*
Verbal	Expressive Goals: Increase mean-length of utterance adjective + noun (purple balloon) Sentence strip: I like to (verb phrase) in the (season).

Surprise Bag

sun	moon	star
sol	*luna*	*estrella*

cloud	rainbow	rain
nube	*arco iris*	*lluvia*

snow	wind	winter
nieve	*viento*	*invierno*

spring	summer	fall
primavera	*verano*	*otoño*

Surprise Bag Sentence Strip

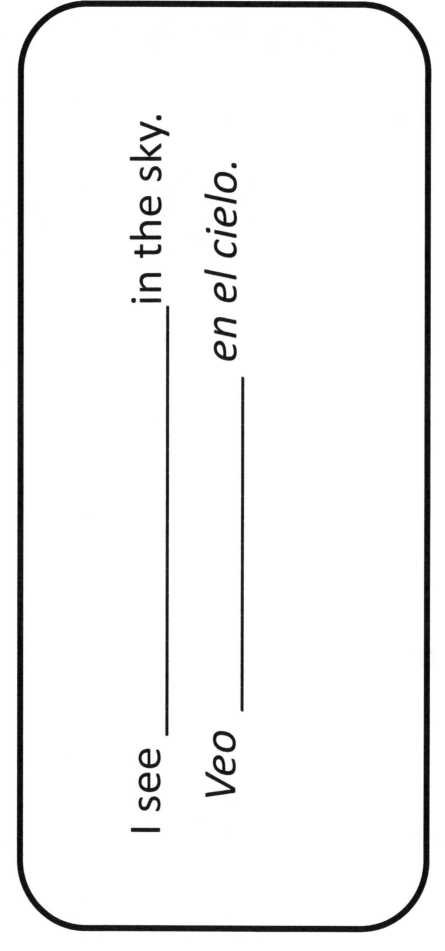

I see _____ in the sky.

Veo _____ en el cielo.

Surprise Bag Sentence Strip

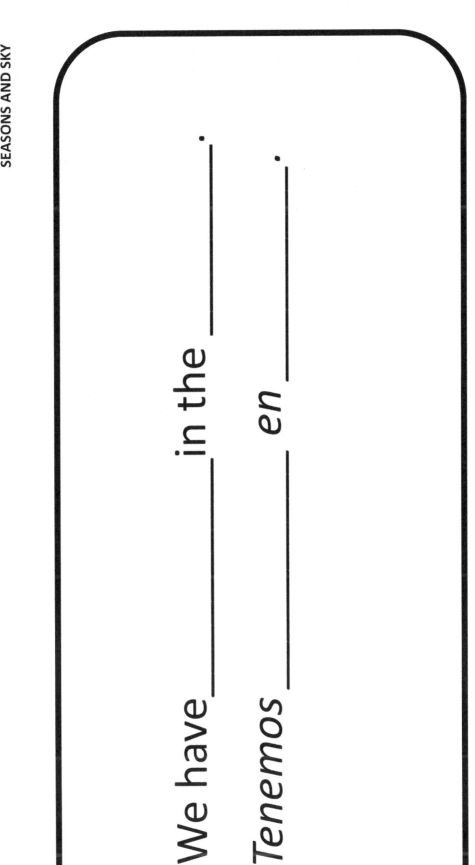

We have _____ in the _____ .

Tenemos _____ en _____ .

6 SEASONS AND SKY

wear a hat and gloves	build a snowman	drink hot chocolate
plant a garden	pick flowers	fly a kite
go swimming	go to the beach	eat popsicles
rake leaves	play football	decorate pumpkins
wear shorts	wear a costume	go to school

English Sentence Strip

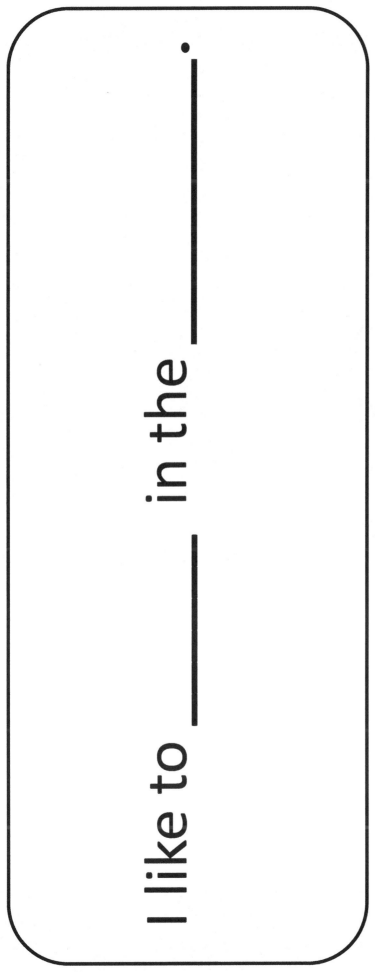

I like to _____ in the _____.

Spanish Sentence Strip Visuals

ponerme gorra y guantes	construir un muñeco de nieve	tomar chocolate
plantar un jardín	recoger flores	volar un papalote
nadar	ir a la playa	comer paletas
recoger hojas	jugar fútbol	decorar calabazas
llevar pantalones cortos	llevar un disfraz	asistir la escuela

Spanish Sentence Strip

Me gusta _____ en .

fall

otoño

spring

primavera

summer

verano

winter

invierno

Song

6 **SEASONS AND SKY**

Song Activity: *Months of the Year/Meses del año*

Suggested goals to target:

- Labeling months of the year

- Sequencing

- Categorizing months into seasons

Purpose:

- Use attached visual cues.

- Teach vocabulary/concepts prior to the song, reinforce concepts during the song, and review concepts after the song.

- Identify and label targeted vocabulary when learning the song's lyrics.

- Ask and answer Wh– questions, such as, "When is (holiday)?"

- Identify and/or label sequencing concepts, such as "First/last."

- Encourage and facilitate participation in group activities.

- Increase and maintain attention to group activities.

Suggested activities:

- Review sequencing of the song with entire class by pointing to months of the year (e.g. "January, February, March...").

- Cut out months, laminate and place Velcro on pictures of seasons in order for students to be able to select an answer to the question, "When is it winter time?" "What season is it in January?'" Ideally, months should go around the seasons in a circular pattern indicating continuity.

Song

Song Activity: *Months of the Year/Meses del año*

January	enero
February	febrero
March	marzo
April	abril
May	mayo
June	junio
July	julio
August	agosto
September	septiembre
October	octubre
November	noviembre
December	diciembre

Question of the Day 1

?

like

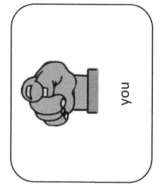

you

night

do

day

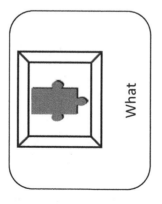

What

La pregunta del día 1

Qué

te

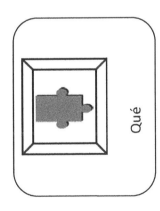

gusta

día

noche

Story 1 / Cuento 1

What do you see in the sky?

¿Qué es lo que ves en el cielo?

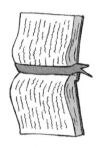

Up in the sky, up in the sky, I spy with my little eye...a bird.

The red bird flies high in the sky.

Arriba en el cielo, arriba en el cielo, con mis ojitos yo veo...un pájaro. El pájaro rojo vuela alto en el cielo.

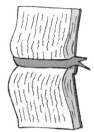

205

Up in the sky, up in the sky, I spy with my little eye...an airplane.

The white plane takes off into the sky.

Arriba en el cielo, arriba en el cielo, con mis ojitos yo veo...el avión. El avión blanco despega hacia el cielo.

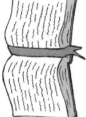

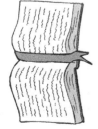

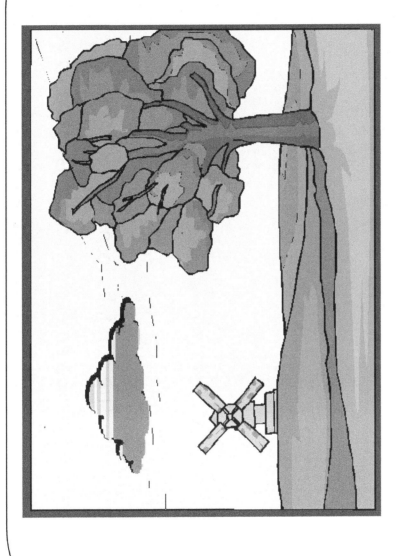

Up in the sky, up in the sky, I spy with my little eye...a cloud.

The gray cloud moves across the sky.

Arriba en el cielo, arriba en el cielo, con mis ojitos yo veo...una nube. La nube gris se mueve por todo el cielo.

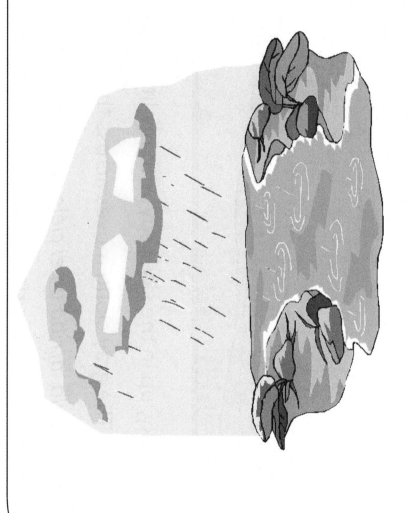

Up in the sky, up in the sky, I spy with my little eye...rain.

The rain falls from the sky.

Arriba en el cielo, arriba en el cielo, con mis ojitos yo veo...lluvia.

La lluvia cae del cielo.

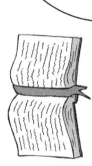

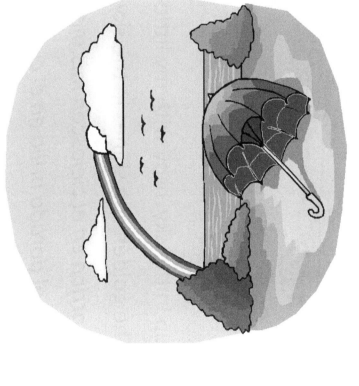

Up in the sky, up in the sky, I spy with my little eye...a rainbow.
The colorful rainbow appears in the sky after the rain.

Arriba en el cielo, arriba en el cielo, con mis ojitos yo veo...un arco iris. El arco iris colorado aparece en el cielo después de la lluvia.

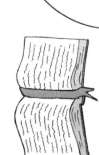

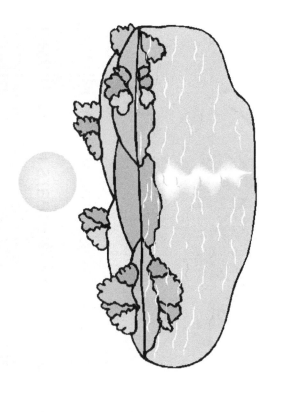

Up in the sky, up in the sky, I spy with my little eye...the sun.

The golden sun shines in the sky.

Arriba en el cielo, arriba en el cielo, con mis ojitos yo veo...el sol.

El sol dorado brilla en el cielo.

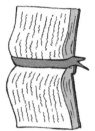

Up in the sky, up in the sky, I spy with my little eye...the moon.

The white moon reflects light in the sky.

Arriba en el cielo, arriba en el cielo, con mis ojitos yo veo...la luna. La luna blanca refleja la luz en el cielo.

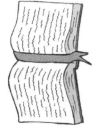

Up in the sky, up in the sky, I spy with my little eye...the stars.

The yellow stars sparkle in the night sky.

Arriba en el cielo, arriba en el cielo, con mis ojitos yo veo...las estrellas. Las estrellas amarillas resplandecen en el cielo.

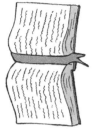

Up in the sky, up in the sky, I spy with my little eye...a rocket ship! The silver rocket ship shoots up in the sky.

Arriba en el cielo, arriba en el cielo, con mis ojitos yo veo... ¡un cohete! El cohete plateado sale disparado hacia el cielo.

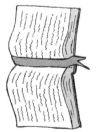

The End

El fin

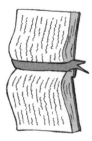

In the sky

balloon	sky	float	see
bird	eye	fly	shine
cloud	airplane	water	tree
rainbow	rain	star	day
moon	sun	rocket	night

—
you
up
down
in

En el cielo

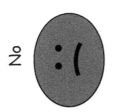

No :(

Sí :)

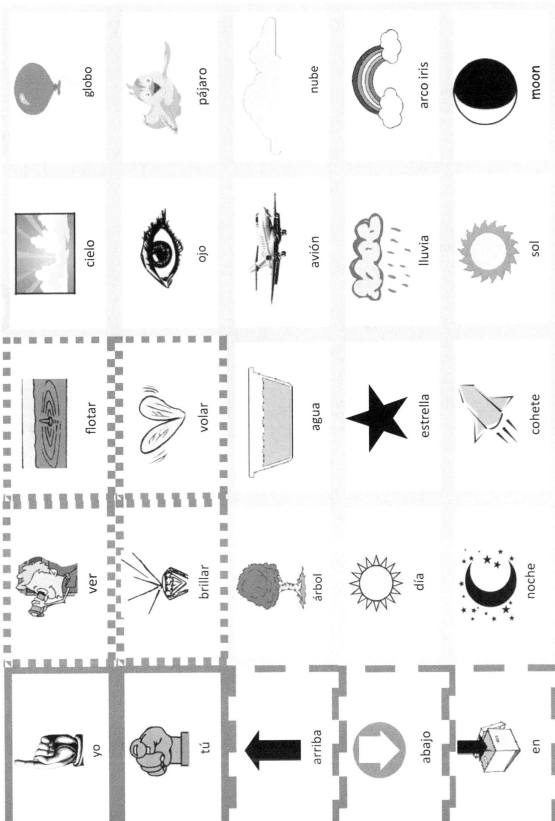

globo

pájaro

nube

arco iris

moon

cielo

ojo

avión

lluvia

sol

flotar

volar

agua

estrella

cohete

ver

brillar

árbol

día

noche

yo

tú

arriba

abajo

en

Story Questions 1

What do you see in the sky?

1. What flies in the sky?

cloud

bird

car

2. When do you see stars?

day

rainbow

night

3. What is wet and falls from the sky?

rain

balloon

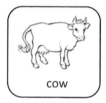
cow

4. What is colorful and comes out after the rain?

rocket ship

rainbow

cloud

5. Where are clouds?

sky

tree

water

Story Questions 1

What do you see in the sky?

1. What flies in the sky?

2. When do you see stars?

3. What is wet and falls from the sky?

4. What is colorful and comes out after the rain?

5. Where are clouds?

Preguntas del cuento 1

¿Qué es lo que ves en el cielo?

1. ¿Que vuela en el cielo?

 nube

 pájaro

 carro

2. ¿Cuando salen las estrellas?

 día

 arco iris

 noche

3. ¿Qué es mojado y cae del cielo?

 lluvia

 globo

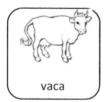 vaca

4. ¿Que tiene muchos colores y sale después de la lluvia?

 cohete

 arco iris

 nube

5. ¿Dónde están las nubes?

 cielo

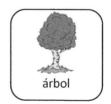 árbol

 agua

Preguntas del cuento 1

SEASONS AND SKY

¿Qué es lo que ves en el cielo?

1. ¿Qué vuela en el cielo?

2. ¿Cuándo salen las estrellas?

3. ¿Qué es mojado y cae del cielo?

4. ¿Qué tiene muchos colores y sale después de la lluvia?

5. ¿Dónde están las nubes?

English Articulation Words

Story 1: What do you see in the sky?

6 SEASONS AND SKY

English

M moon, my, moves

P purple, plane, appears, airplane, up, ship

B balloon, bird, rainbow

K rocket, takes, sky, sparkle, across, reflects, colorful, cloud

G gray, golden

T rocket, takes, after, little, light, night, white

D bird, red, cloud

F after, falls, from, reflects, colorful, flies, floats

S sun, silver, falls, stars, takes, sky, spy, sparkle

L little, colorful, blue, cloud, flies, floats, plane, reflects

R red, rain, rainbow, rocket, gray, from, across, through, reflects, colorful

---

Sonidos del habla—Español

Cuento 1: *¿Qué es lo que ves en el cielo?*

6 SEASONS AND SKY

Spanish

M mis, mueva, morado, amarillas

P por, pájaro, despega, dispara

B ves, veo, vuela, arriba, avión, nube, lluvia

K caer, que, cohete, arco iris, blanco

N avión, nube, luna, lucen, blanco

T alto, ojitos, cohete

D despega, dispara, morado, dorado, plateada

F refleja, flota

S cielo, sol, azul, arco iris, estrellas, amarillas

L luz, luna, lucen, cielo, sol, blanco, globo, flota, refleja, plateada

R rojo, refleja, arco iris, dorado, pájaro, brilla, gris

Question of the Day 2

season

favorite

you

? .

What

is

spring

summer

fall

winter

La pregunta del día 2

¿?

favorita	estación	tu	Cuál

es

¿?

otoño	verano	primavera	invierno

6 — SEASONS AND SKY

Story 2 / Cuento 2

The Four Seasons

Las cuatro estaciones

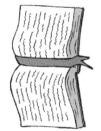

We do many things during winter, spring, summer, fall. What season is it?
These are the four seasons in a year.

Hacemos muchas cosas durante el invierno, la primavera, el verano, el otoño. Éstas son las cuatro estaciones en el año. ¿Cuál estación es?

It's cold, there's ice and snow on the ground outside, it's winter!

Hace mucho frío, hay hielo y nieve en la tierra afuera, es invierno!

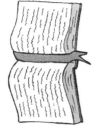

In winter we bundle up, build snowmen, and drink hot chocolate.

*En el invierno, nos abrigamos bien, hacemos muñecos de nieve,
y tomamos chocolate.*

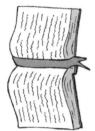

There are four seasons in a year. What season comes next?

Hay cuatro estaciones en el año. ¿Cuál estación sigue?

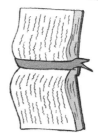

It's rainy and warm, grass is growing and flowers are blooming...it's spring!

Está lloviendo y hace más calor, el pasto está creciendo y las flores están saliendo... es primavera!

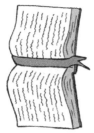

In the spring, we plant a garden, pick flowers and fly a kite.

En la primavera, plantamos un jardín, recogemos flores y volamos un papalote.

There are four seasons in a year. What season comes next?

Hay cuatro estaciones en el año. ¿Cuál estación sigue?

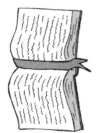

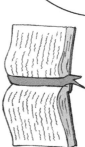

It's very hot outside, the sun is shining and we are on vacation...it's summer!

Hace mucho calor, el sol está brillando y estamos de vacaciones! ¡Es verano!

In the summer, we go swimming and eat ice cream.

En el verano, nadamos y comemos helado.

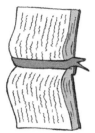

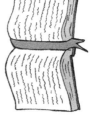

There are four seasons in a year. What season comes next?

Hay cuatro estaciones en el año. ¿Cuál estación sigue?

It's windy and cool outside. The leaves are changing colors and falling from the trees. It's fall!

Hay viento y hace fresco afuera. Las hojas están cambiando de color y se están cayendo de los árboles. ¡Es otoño!

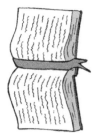

In the fall, we rake leaves, play football outside and decorate pumpkins.

En otoño, recogemos hojas, jugamos futbol afuera y decoramos calabazas.

The End

El fin

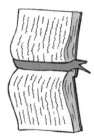

The Four Seasons

 No

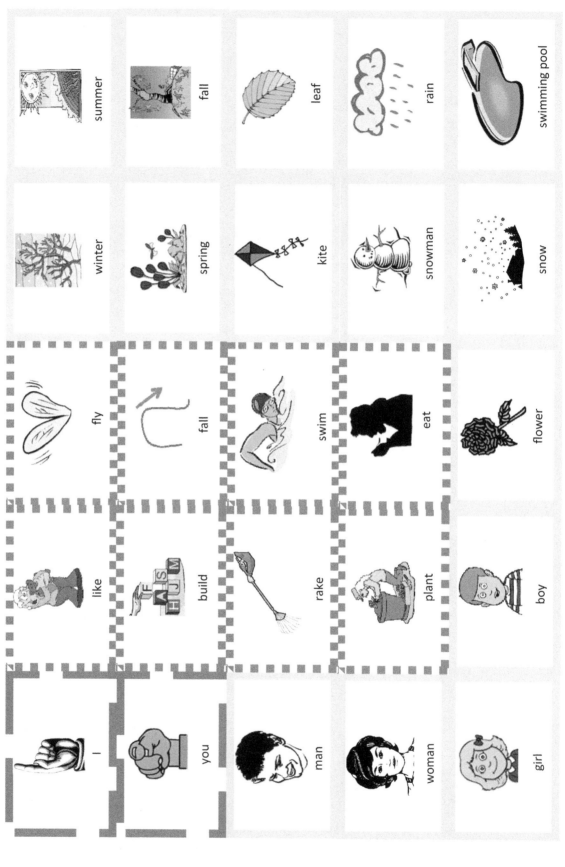 Yes

summer	winter	fly	like	I
fall	spring	fall	build	you
leaf	kite	swim	rake	man
rain	snowman	eat	plant	woman
swimming pool	snow	flower	boy	girl

Las cuatro estaciones

No :(

Sí :)

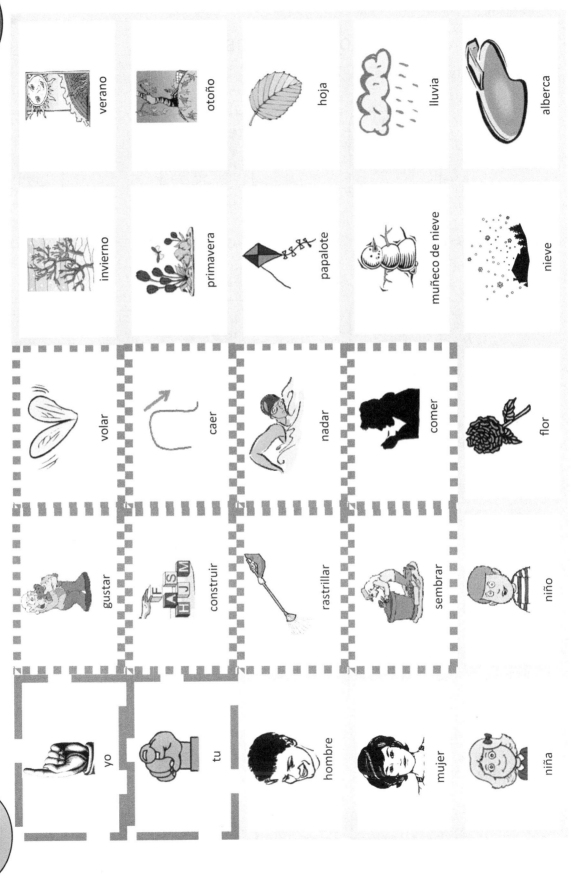

verano

otoño

hoja

lluvia

alberca

invierno

primavera

papalote

muñeco de nieve

nieve

volar

caer

nadar

comer

flor

gustar

construir

rastrillar

sembrar

niño

yo

tu

hombre

mujer

niña

Story Questions 2

The Four Seasons

6

SEASONS AND SKY

1. When is it very hot outside?

fall

spring

summer

2. When do flowers bloom?

winter

spring

summer

3. When can we see snow on the ground?

winter

summer

fall

4. When do the leaves fall off the trees?

fall

winter

spring

5. Which one is NOT a season?

summer

fall

rain

Story Questions 2

The Four Seasons

1. When is it very hot outside?

2. When do flowers bloom?

3. When can we see snow on the ground?

4. When do the leaves fall off the trees?

5. Which one is NOT a season?

Preguntas del cuento 1

6 SEASONS AND SKY

Las cuatro estaciones

1. ¿Cuándo hace mucho calor?

otoño

primavera

verano

2. ¿Cuándo crecen las flores?

invierno

primavera

verano

3. ¿Cuándo podemos ver nieve en el suelo?

invierno

verano

otoño

4. ¿Cuándo caen las hojas de los árboles?

otoño

invierno

primavera

5. ¿Cuál NO es una estación?

verano

otoño

lluvia

Preguntas del cuento 1

6

SEASONS AND SKY

Las cuatro estaciones

1. ¿Cuándo hace mucho calor?

2. ¿Cuándo crecen las flores?

3. ¿Cuándo podemos ver nieve en el suelo?

4. ¿Cuándo caen las hojas de los árboles?

5. ¿Cuál NO es una estación?

English Articulation Words

Story 2: The Four Seasons

English

M   blooming, pumpkins, warm, comes, cream, pumpkins, swimming, from, summer, snowmen, cream

P   pick, pumpkins, play, plant

B   build, bundle, blooming

K   kite, cool, cold, colors, comes, cream, pumpkins, pick

G   go, garden, grass, growing, ground, things, spring, during, swimming

T   we, what, warm, winter, windy

D   do, during, drink, decorate, build, ground, cold, windy, outside

F   fall, football, four, falling, fly, flowers, from

S   sun, summer, seasons, snow, spring, snowmen, swimming, outside, ice, grass

L   leaves, chocolate, cool, fall, fly, blooming, play, plant, flowers

R   rake, rainy, very, warm, during, garden, are, summer, year, winter, colors, flowers, drink, cream, ground, grass, growing

Sonidos del habla—Español

Cuento 2: *Las cuatro estaciones*

6 SEASONS AND SKY

Spanish

M más, **m**ucho, **m**uchas, **m**uñeco, to**m**a**m**os, co**m**en, pri**m**avera, ca**m**biando

P pasto, plantamos, papalote, primavera

B verano, volamos, vacaciones, brillando, invierno, abrigamos, árboles, nieve

K cosas, creciendo, cuatro, comemos, cual, cambiando, calor, cayendo, color, calabazas, vacaciones, muñeco, decorar

N nieve, nadamos, plantamos, verano, brillando, creciendo

T tomamos, otoño, pasto, plantamos, papalote, cuatro, fútbol, estás, estaciones, tierra

D decorar, lloviendo, brillando, cayendo, brillando, cambiando, creciendo, nadamos, saliendo, jardín, helado

F frío, fresco, fútbol, flores, afuera

S sol, estás, estaciones, saliendo, sigue, hace, hacemos, pasto, más, cosas, flores

L la, helado, hielo, papalote, color, volamos, calabazas, el, cual, sol, plantamos, flores

R recoger, afuera, flores, jardín, tierra, calor, jugar, decorar, primavera, frío, brillando, fresco, creciendo, cuatro, invierno

Game: Seasons and the Sky Bingo

rainbow

flower

winter

sun

spring

rain

fall

snow

summer

Game: Seasons and the Sky Bingo

flower

rain

fall

snow

spring

sun

summer

rainbow

winter

Game: Seasons and the Sky Bingo

rain

flower

fall

snow

summer

rainbow

winter

sun

spring

Juego: las estaciones y el cielo bingo

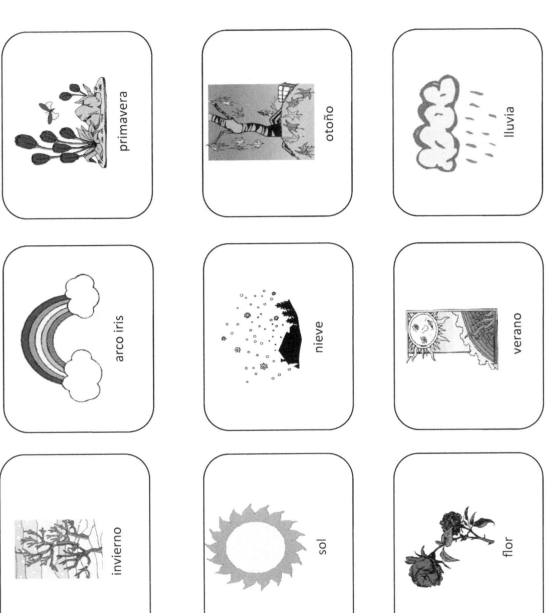

primavera

otoño

lluvia

arco iris

nieve

verano

invierno

sol

flor

251

Juego: las estaciones y el cielo bingo

nieve

primavera

verano

otoño

sol

lluvia

flor

invierno

arco iris

Juego: las estaciones y el cielo bingo

lluvia	verano	sol
invierno	flor	otoño
arco iris	nieve	primavera

Craft Activity: Finger-paint rainbow

1.  Choose a color

first

2. Dip your finger in the paint gently

3. Press same color in the circle on the paper

4. Put 1 drop of glue on the cotton ball

5. Paste cotton balls under the rainbow for the clouds

last

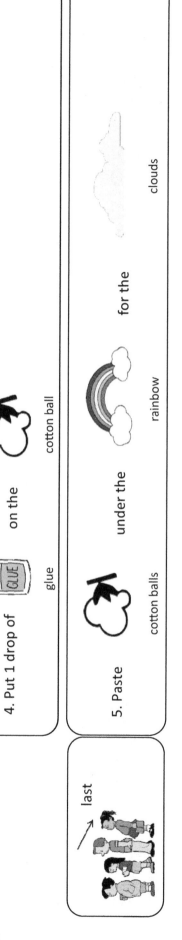

Actividad de arte: arco iris de huellas digitales

primero

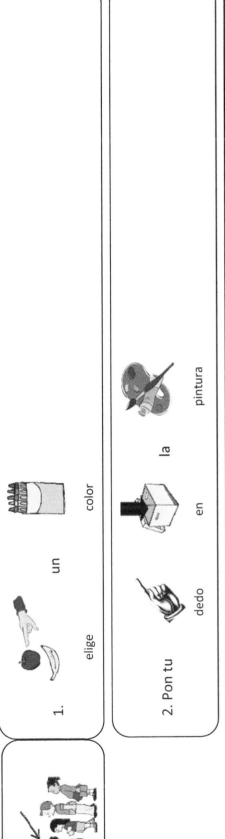

1. elige un color

2. Pon tu dedo en la pintura

3. Oprime tu dedo en el círculo del mismo color

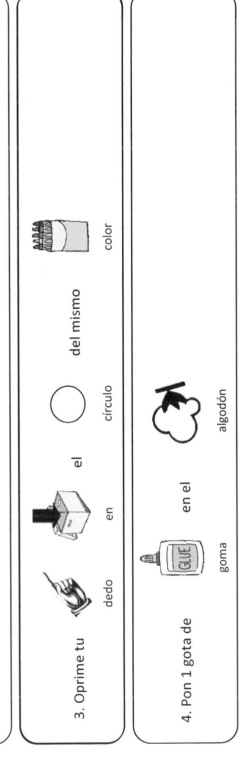

4. Pon 1 gota de goma en el algodón

5. Pega el algodón debajo del arco iris para las nubes

al final

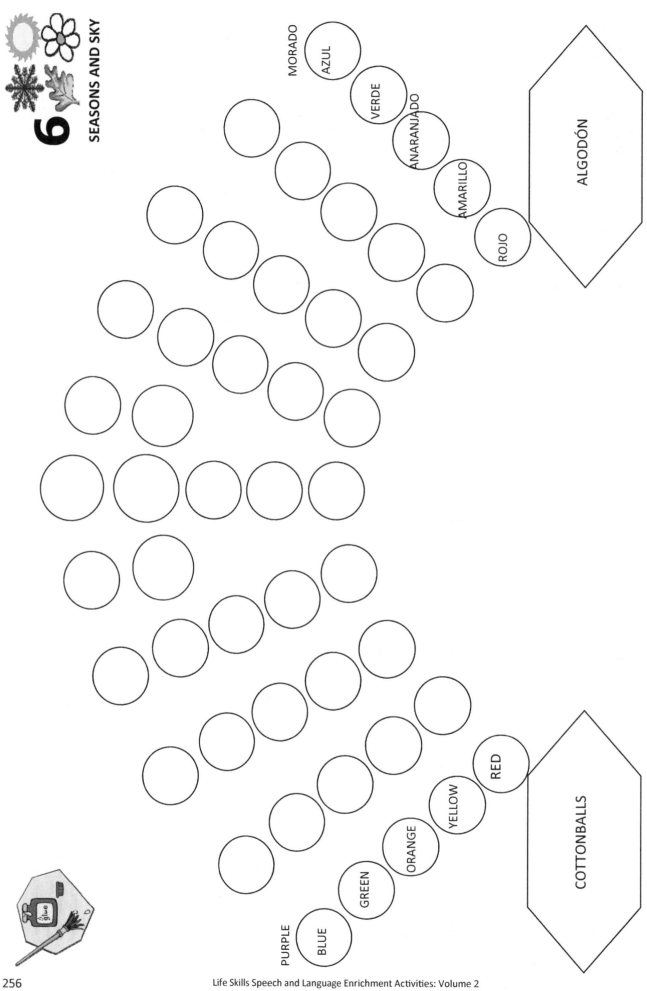

6 SEASONS AND SKY

ALGODÓN

MORADO
AZUL
VERDE
ANARANJADO
AMARILLO
ROJO

COTTONBALLS

PURPLE
BLUE
GREEN
ORANGE
YELLOW
RED

Recipe: Hot Chocolate for a Cold Day

first

1. pour — the — milk — in — the — cup

2. Add 2 — spoons — of — chocolate — to the — cup

3. stir — the — milk

4. Put the — cup — in — the — microwave — for about 30 seconds

5. Add 5 — marshmallows — to the — cup

last

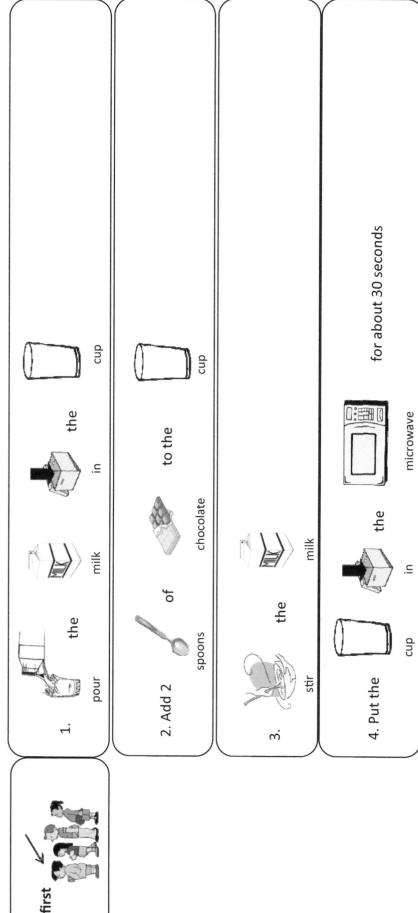

*To make chocolate milk: follow steps 1-3. Compare hot/cold.

Receta: Chocolate caliente para un día frío

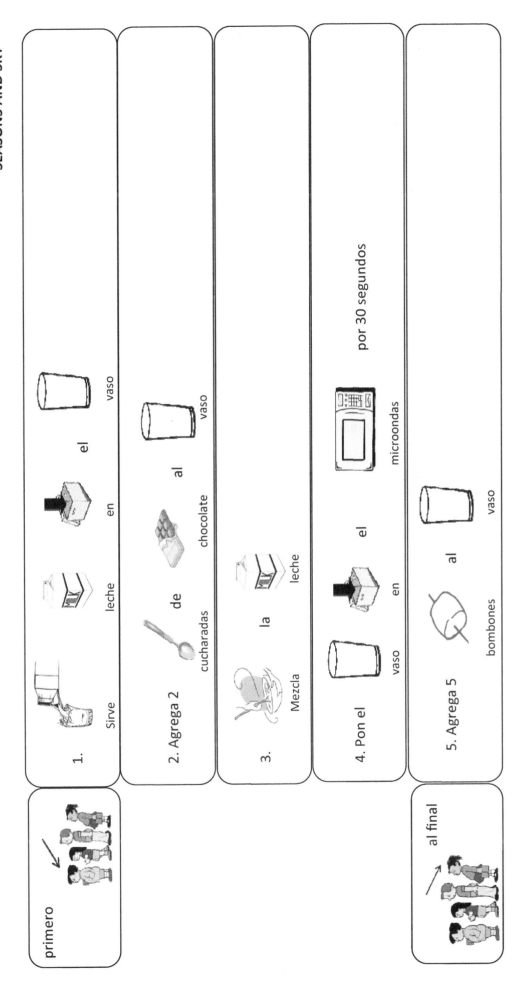

primero

1. Sirve leche en el vaso

2. Agrega 2 cucharadas de chocolate al vaso

3. Mezcla la leche chocolate

4. Pon el vaso en el microondas por 30 segundos

5. Agrega 5 bombones al vaso

al final

*Para chocolate frío: Sigue pasos 1-3. Compare caliente/frío.

REFERENCES

ASHA guidelines. Retrieved August 1, 2014, from: http://www.asha.org/public/speech/disorders/lbld.htm#d.

Bolderson, S., Dosanjh, C., Milligan, C., Pring, T. & Chiat, S. (2011). Colourful semantics: A clinical investigation. *Child Language Teaching and Therapy 27*(3), 344-353.

Cuomo, A. M., (2012) "Niall Toner, MA, BCBA Conducting Preference Assessments on Individuals with Autism and other Developmental Disabilities."

Curriculum and Instructional Materials. (n.d.). Retrieved June 20, 2015, from http;//tea.texas.gov/Curriculum_and_Instructional_Programs/

Ebbels, S. (2007). Teaching grammar to school-aged children with specific language impairment using shape coding. *Child Learning Teaching and Therapy 23(*1), 67-93.

Fey, M.E., Long, S.H., & Finestack, L.H. (2003). Ten principles of grammar facilitation for children with specific language impairments. *American Journal of Speech-Language Pathology* 12, 3-15.

Hume, K. (2009). Visual schedules: How and why to use them in the classroom. *Autism-Society.org*. Retrieved August 4, 2014 from: http://www.education.com/reference/article/visual-schedule-classroom-autism-ASD/.

Jensen, Eric. Teaching with poverty in mind: What being poor does to kids' brains and what schools can do about it. ASCD, 2009.

Leinhardt, G., Weidman, C., & Hammond, K. M. (1987). Introduction and integration of classroom routines by expert teachers. *Curriculum Inquiry*, 135-176.

Liboiron, N., & Soto, G. (2006). Shared storybook reading with a student who uses alternative and augmentative communication: A description of scaffolding practices. Child Language Teaching and Therapy, 22(1), 69-95.

McGinty, A.S. & Justice, L.M. (2006) Classroom-based versus pull-out language intervention: An examination of the experimental evidence. EBP Briefs, 1, 1.

McGregor, G., & Vogelsberg, R. T. (1998). Inclusive schooling practices: Pedagogical and research foundations: A synthesis of literature that informs best practices about inclusive schooling. Pittsburgh, PA: Allegheny University of the Health Sciences.

Paquette, A., & Rieg, S. (2008) Using music to support the literacy development of young English language learners. *Early Childhood Education Journal 36*, 227-232.

Throneburg, R.N., Calvert, L.K., Sturm, J.J., Paramboukas, A.A., & Paul, P.J. (2000). A comparison of service delivery models: Effects on curricular vocabulary skills in the school setting. *American Journal of Speech-Language Pathology 9*, 10-20.

Van Kleeck, A., Schwarz, A., Fey, M., Kaiser, A., Miller, J., & Weitzman, E. (2010). Should we use telegraphic or grammatical input in the early stages of language development with children who have language impairments? A meta-analysis of the research and expert opinion. *American Journal of Speech-Language Pathology, 19*, 3-21.

Whalen, C., & Schreibman, L. (2003). Joint attention trainging for children with autism using behavior modification procedures. Journal of Child Psychology and Psychiatry, 44(3), 456-468.

Whitehurst, G.J. & Lonigan, C.J. (2003). Emergent literacy: Development from prereaders to readers, in Handbook of Early Literacy Research, Volume 1, Susan Neuman and David Dickinson (Eds.). New York: Guilford.

Wilcox, M. J., Kouri, T.A., & Caswell, S. B. (1991). Early language intervention: A comparison of classroom and individual treatment. *American Journal of Speech-Language Pathology, 1*, 49-60.

Yoder, P.J., Spruytenburg, H., Edwards, A., & Davies, B. (January 1995) Effect of verbal routine contexts and expansions on gains in the mean length of utterance in children with developmental delays. *Language, Speech, and Hearing Services in Schools 26,* 21-32.

Made in the USA
Columbia, SC
02 October 2018